Dire Straits

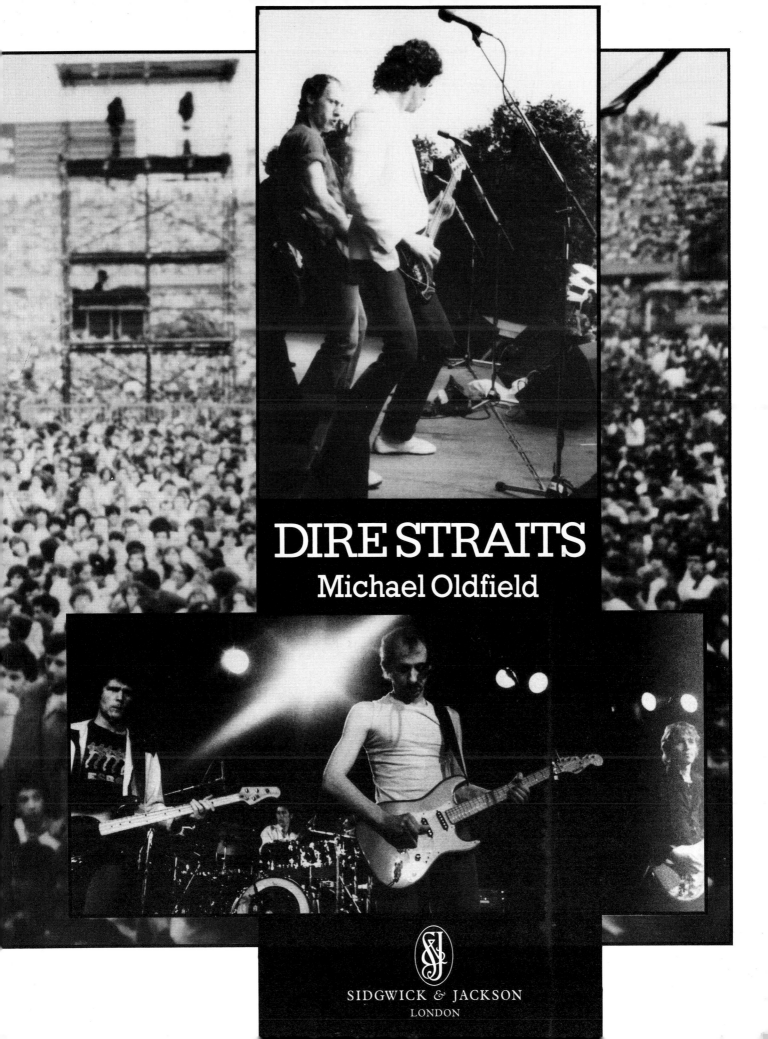

DIRE STRAITS
Michael Oldfield

SIDGWICK & JACKSON
LONDON

First published in 1984 in Great Britain
by Sidgwick and Jackson Limited

Copyright © 1984 by Michael Oldfield

Designed by Ray Hyden

ISBN 0-283-98990-4 (hardcover)
     0-283-98995-5 (softcover)

Origination by Type Generation Limited
Printed by The Garden City Press Limited,
Letchworth, Hertfordshire SG6 1JS
for Sidgwick and Jackson Limited
1 Tavistock Chambers, Bloomsbury Way
London WC1A 2SG

Contents

CHAPTER 1
Behind the Lines

What the tour manager sees: Kevin Jones waits to lead Dire Straits back to the dressing-rooms after a 1981 show in Italy

'A lovestruck Romeo sings a streetsuss serenade'

It's a freezing December evening in London, and small knots of people, huddled deep in winter coats, spiral up the hill from Wembley Park underground station. They gather in the parade ground outside Wembley Arena, faces pinched with cold, feet stamping away the rising frost, breath streaming away like smoke in the icy air.

The billboard reads: 'Dire Straits. December 18, 19, 20, 21. Sold out'. Touts flit from group to group offering tickets at up to five times the face value. Hands nervously pat pockets to ensure the precious paper is still there; eyes glance surreptitiously at small print and confirm that the doors should have opened ten minutes ago.

Inside the entrance security men, arms folded resolutely over beribboned chests, stand guard over turnstiles, waiting to click in tonight's audience. In the horseshoe thoroughfare that flanks the seating area, shops and stalls are ready for business. Beer taps drip, frankfurters bob in steaming water, and Dire Straits T-shirts sit in neat piles, stacked in order of size.

Inside the auditorium itself, tiers of empty seats banked up on three sides stare bleakly down on to the central area. Security men in orange Day-Glo jackets are dotted around, watching the stage with desultory interest. At the far end, two desks face the stage, one controlling the lights, the other the sound. It's from the latter that Pete Granger, Dire Straits' sound engineer, announces over the PA system: 'It's absolutely essential that we run through again!' There is desperation in his voice.

On-stage, marooned amongst tons of equipment, miles of cable and thousands of pounds' worth of instruments, Dire Straits await a decision. Centre back, behind his drumkit, is Terry Williams, flanked by Tommy Mandel on his left and Alan Clark on his right, both surrounded by keyboards.

On the stage proper stand three guitarists. Below Tommy is Hal Lindes, earnestly discussing his guitar with a roadie. Below Alan is John Illsley, leaning against a riser and keeping his bass ticking over with the odd strum. To John's right is sax player Mel Collins, waiting patiently as his mike is adjusted to the correct height. Mel is playing on 'Two Young Lovers' at the Wembley shows, and it's this number that has yet to be checked.

Stage centre, Mark Knopfler, manager Ed Bicknell and tour manager Paul Cummins are deciding whether to run through the song once more or to let the audience in. Music wins out – it always does with Dire Straits – and 'Two Young Lovers' blasts out across thousands of empty seats as the final touches are put to the technical side of the show.

Finally, the doors are opened and the frozen fans allowed in. Musicians and roadies clamber off the stage and disappear into the safety of their backstage world. Security is tight here, with guards on all exits and entrances; only those with special plastic photo passes can reach this area. Even distinguished visitors have to be led down through the VIP section by a pass-holder.

Exactly who these distinguished visitors are is currently being worked out in the promoter's office, where Ed and Paul are scanning the guest list.

'He can have a ticket for the VIP box, but no way is he coming into the dressing room,' says Ed of a well-known rock star. 'Last time he came backstage he got hold of Mark and bored him to death for an hour.'

They work their way through the list, weeding out hangers-on from musicians, visitors, old friends and relatives the band would genuinely like to see after the show, interrupted every now and then by a crew member hopeful for a spare ticket for a girlfriend who's arrived unexpectedly.

Backstage, Wembley is very spacious – unlike the facilities at some venues on this tour where the touring party of around forty people have been crammed into a couple of tiny rooms. Here, the crew have their own dining-room, where Lorraine Taylor, the cook who is now a permanent fixture on Dire Straits tours, dispenses hot meals throughout the day.

It's a long day for her, starting with breakfast as the crew move in to set up the equipment and ending with dinner for the band after the show. In between, meals run into one another as one section of the crew works while the other eats. Then she packs up her cooker, fridge, food, pans and crockery into one of the trucks for hauling on to the next gig.

In the band's dressing-room, through a corridor flanked with yet more security guards, there's a noticeable buzz in the air – everyone's looking forward to the four Wembley shows, the culmination of three weeks of British dates. Kevin Jones, who looks after the band on the road, is checking the stage clothes. Liz, Ed's secretary, is ironing Tommy's purple suit while its owner takes a shower. Terry is bouncing his daughter on his knee. Mel is telling Mark about a tour he's just completed with jazz saxophonist Gato Barbieri.

The survivors: Mark Knopfler and John Illsley, founder Straits, at Wembley Arena, December 1982

. . . And a big hand for Hal Lindes. End-of-tour prank, Christmas 1982

12

It's John who voices the only note of concern: exactly what end-of-tour pranks are the crew going to play on the band?

'I've told them,' says Mark, 'they can do anything they like as long as it doesn't interfere with the music.'

Inevitably, memories are jogged about the practical jokes that have been played on them. John recalls the last night of the first American tour, in Sacramento in 1979.

'We were playing "Once Upon A Time In The West" and we heard this ringing off-stage. We all looked round and ignored it at first, but then one of the crew walked on with a telephone and gave it to Mark. He picked it up and what they'd done was connect it to the mixing desk so everything was coming out over the PA system. Mark picked up the phone and said "Hello", and this incredibly sexy girl's voice said: "Mark, what are you doing after the show tonight?" We all burst out laughing.'

'What about that last night we played the Rainbow,' says Mark, 'when Lorraine came on with cups of tea for everyone? Then another time she came on with a full meal?'

Terry remembers the last night of a Meat Loaf tour. 'As I went on-stage, I saw out of the corner of my eye the stage manager put this big custard pie on my seat. So when I walked up to the kit, without him seeing I put the pie on the floor, and when I sat down I made this awful face as though I'd just sat on it. Big laugh from the side of the stage. Then halfway through the show I called him over, and when he came over, I shoved the pie, splat, right in his face. I've never seen anyone so surprised in my whole life.'

The stories are now fair flying around the room: the rubber brick that earlier that day had been dropped on Pete Granger's mixing desk, causing heart palpitations for the sound man . . . the smoke bomb that was put in Alan's piano . . . the can-can chorus line of crew members that high-kicked its way across the stage during 'Les Boys' one night . . .

A huge roar from the crowd indicates that the house lights have gone down. Leading the way with a lighted torch tracking the white arrows painted on the floor, Paul Cummins takes the band around the back of the stage and points the way up the steps. From this moment Dire Straits are on their own.

To anyone familiar only with the records, the pull and power of Dire Straits on-stage comes as a shock. Above all, they are a *rock* band, and they can beat it out with the best of the high-energy groups. But they never resort to the clichéd tricks of the rabble-rousers who reduce songs to repetitive riffs and elongate them with pretentious solos.

The songs themselves are the most important element of their music, and everything is tailored to fit them. They're complex creations, each with an emotional life of its own. On record, the songs are portraits, descriptions, words and music. On-stage they live and breathe.

Tonight, the audience is completely immersed in the ebb and flow of emotion pouring from the stage, adrift on the tide of music. From the opening chords of 'Once Upon A Time In The West', the lushness of the keyboard instrumentation and the throbbing riff wash out to all four corners of the arena.

13

A teasing break with 'Industrial Disease', light and jokey, before the power chords of 'Expresso Love' crack out of Mark's guitar and ricochet across the auditorium, his solos taken in short bursts and built into the songs rather than flying off into ten-minute side trips, his voice hot with urgency and feeling.

They slow it down. 'It Never Rains' begins gently enough but builds and builds, the song constructed with a whole range of dynamics, the pace elastic. Instrumentally, Dire Straits are a group of voices holding a conversation. They never all try to speak at once, but create a background buzz as talk flits from one instrument to another. The intro to 'Romeo And Juliet' earns a huge cheer of familiarity from the crowd, and then they go into 'Love Over Gold', completing a trilogy of songs that chart an affair that went wrong, a love that gave way to bemused incomprehension that it's over, to bitter recrimination, to belated acceptance. The words are given added poignancy by their delivery. No smooth balladeer uttering words without feeling, Mark Knopfler is the untrained, unpolished voice of the ordinary man.

The pulsebeat of 'Private Investigations' starts up, heartbreaks and heartaches shrugged off in the inexorable climb to a new emotional high, culminating in a battle between the seductive chords of Alan's piano and the ruthless venom of the electric guitar.

'You get a shiver in the dark . . .' Mark (left) and John, Wembley

The sultans of swing: Mark and John, Wembley

And they're off again, cruising through a cracking 'Sultans Of Swing', lyrics changed to fit the band – 'Check out Guitar Hal/He's my pal/ He knows all the chords . . . And Alan doesn't mind/ He's got a daytime job' – notes spinning from Mark's guitar between each line.

Now fun-time, with 'Twisting By The Pool', Terry and Mark toying with the audience, urging them to shout louder and louder to get the drummer motivated. Then the band tear it up, Tommy twisting away, a purple-clad dervish behind his keyboards.

Out steps Mel Collins for 'Two Young Lovers', a song that's a perfect pastiche of Chuck Berry and which glories in days of innocence, an atmosphere soon shattered as Hal steps out to the front of the stage to wrench a thundering solo from his guitar as he poses, pouts and struts in true eighties metallic style.

They cool down with the gentle lilt of 'Portobello Belle', introduced as 'an Irish reggae song', and air pumps back into lungs before 'Tunnel Of Love', a fairground full of emotional and musical rides. Exciting, exhilarating and exhausting, it just can't be followed. With a wave, Dire Straits leave the stage.

But return they must, with 'Telegraph Road', another all-encompassing number that comes in like a lamb and goes out like a lion, a great blast of thunderflash filling the stage with light and smoke.

Off they troop again, then back once more for 'Solid Rock', an electrifying blast of rock 'n' roll sound, the kind that blisters paint and buckles metal. Finally, they strike up the gentle instrumental theme of 'Going Home', played out as the houselights go up and roadies come on-stage to dismantle equipment. The message is clear: this really is the end . . . for tonight.

But where did it begin? The four nights at Wembley are just part of a twenty-two date British tour, in itself merely the start of a world tour that will last around nine months and take the band to Australia, New Zealand and Japan before winding up in Europe in the summer. In between, hundreds of promotional appearances have to be fitted in, Mark and Alan have to complete the soundtrack to the film *Local Hero* and, at the last minute, time has been found in the schedule to allow Mark to produce the new Bob Dylan album.

The details are worked out in the offices of Damage Management, Ed and Paul's base in Walton Street, South Kensington. Where the band will play is established long before Mark has decided exactly what songs they will be performing.

First, Ed works out a rough itinerary that takes into account everything from the weather – it makes no sense to tour Scandinavia in the winter, while Southern Europe is obviously a good place to play in the summer because local audiences will be boosted by tourists – to the competition: no band wants to follow on the heels of another – there just isn't that much spare money around for tickets these days.

Then the wheeling and dealing begins. Ed, who acts as the band's agent, an art in itself, contacts local promoters who will actually organize the shows, trying to get as large a guarantee for the band as possible. These days, the Straits' pulling power is well-known –

virtually every date they play around the world is sold out – but it wasn't always the case.

Paul remembers: 'We were playing a gig in Germany, in February 1979, and we had the capacity of the hall down as 3,500. It was the kind of place that you can curtain off to make it as big or as small as you want . . . it could be 1,500 or 6,000.

'In advance, we'd done 2,100 tickets, so we realized that we needed a big walk-up on the night to fill out the 3,500 capacity we'd set. In the event, 3,500 people turned up on top of the 2,100 who had tickets. We all looked at each other and said: "Christ, we're going to make a fortune," because anything over 3,000 we were on 90 per cent of the net. The promoter was in tears!'

Dealing with European promoters can have its problems, particularly in Italy, where threats and warnings are part of the way of doing business. 'They say that if you don't do a show with them they'll shoot out the tyres on the bus, or make sure you get held up at the border, or get the local crew to black the gig,' Paul continues. 'It's all connections in Italy – if you don't know the right people, then forget it.'

Europe, at least, is free of union problems, unlike parts of the United States. In New York, for example, the all-powerful Teamsters Union can reduce the hardiest tour manager to tears with demands for overtime or extra payments if a TV interview is filmed in the theatre; they can even exclude the band's crew from the venue during the union lunch-hour.

The biggest headache for setting up tours on a worldwide scale is the multiplicity of different rules and regulations that apply, not only from country to country, but from town to town. For instance, truck

Above: Solid Rock. Mel Collins gives a saxy punch to the classic Straits rocker

18

permits are compulsory in Switzerland in order to travel overnight on Saturdays. Foreign artist tax laws in Austria mean that a full deduction of expenses is not possible unless the band plays a series of dates, thus allowing it to qualify as a travelling show. And everywhere the complicated bye-laws and ordinances pertaining to safety govern where extinguishers are positioned, the inspection of lighting trusses that hang from the ceiling, even what kind of bulb is used in lamps.

Much of this can be left to promoters, of course, although safety is a high priority for the band. They won't use fly-by-night operators who offer huge sums of money but put the audience at risk.

Paul: 'You always have to remember that disasters can and do happen. Each gig is a potential riot. There could be a fire, and you've got to make sure that thousands of people can get out of the place. There's a great deal of responsibility and if anything goes wrong, it's the band who will be blamed.'

Not all regulations, however, are apparently sensible. Some sort of prize ought to be awarded to the Greater London Council, who needed to know whether the band would have anything resembling a phallic symbol on-stage before permission was granted for the Wembley shows to go ahead.

Wait for it: Mark and Terry Williams take a dramatic pause before the final crashing chords of 'Telegraph Road'

W hile Paul and Ed work out the tour's detailed itinerary, booking hotels, coaches, crew and equipment, the band gather at their rehearsal studio, the Wood Wharf in Greenwich. Perched on the southern bank of a serpentine twist in the River Thames, it's an ideal situation. There are no neighbours to disturb in this wasteland of deserted warehouses and derelict buildings.

On a summer's afternoon, the view from the studio windows takes in the sweep of the river: Barges chug by, roped together in packs, rusty freighters ply their trade and glass-topped cruisers carry tourists up and down from the *Cutty Sark*. But on a cold November night, the water is dark and sullen; only an occasional light betrays the presence of traffic.

Dire Straits are shoe-horned into what appears to be no more than a large living-room, but with every spare inch of space packed with instruments and equipment. The floor is alive with electric cables snaking in and out of the gaps between speaker cabinets; mike stands sprout out of the worn carpet.

Mark stands facing the band, a conductor without a baton, transferring the music in his head into the fingers of the players; tutoring new members in the Dire Straits repertoire – neither Terry nor Tommy have played live with the band before; translating record-fresh songs from *Love Over Gold,* the *Local Hero* soundtrack, and the 'Twisting By The Pool' EP into stage terms; reworking old favourites like 'Romeo And Juliet', so they will dance out with renewed vigour and vitality.

Tommy picks out an instrumental frill on one of his keyboards. *Da da dum dum dum dum.*

'That's good, Tommy,' says Mark. 'Try it a little lower.' *Da da dum dum dum dum.*

'I'll try it on this,' says Alan. *Da da dum dum dum dum.*

'No', says Mark, 'Tommy's sounds better. You hold the horns, let

them fade right away.' *Da da dum dum. Da da dum dum.*

'No Tommy, that's not what you did before. Do it like the first time.'
Da da dum dum dum dum.

Tommy runs through it several times; Terry picks up a beat and
formulates a drum pattern to accompany Tommy.

'That's great Terry. Just make it a little softer, and when it ends just
hold off the beat and then come in, crash!'

Terry tries it out, John brings his bass in to join him. Then Mark
and Hal pick up their guitars and they run through it again and again.
This new sequence lasts perhaps twenty seconds; it's taken at least
twenty minutes to get it absolutely right. And so it goes on, every day
for a month, up to twelve hours at a go with a couple of short rest
breaks, each song worked out in painstaking detail.

Finally, songs merge into a set. Pete Granger knows what sounds
to expect; Chas Herington can work out a lighting plan to highlight
the music; the itinerary is finalized. Dire Straits are ready to roll.

November 30, 1982. A gloomy, rainy afternoon in Guildford, a
few short hours away from the real thing. This Civic Hall gig is a kind
of unofficial start to the *Love Over Gold* tour, a proper set that will
also act as a warm-up and pinpoint any problems.

As the band come on-stage for the sound check there's no panic:
the tour machine has slipped easily into gear. And backstage there
are most definitely no first-night nerves. None to be admitted,
anyway. But there is undeniably tension in the air. Musicians talk
without concentrating. 'Yeah,' they all say, 'it's great to be back on
the road after fifteen months' – they eat distractedly, picking at their
food, and wander around, checking everything over in their minds.

And then the moment arrives. They must file up the stairs to face
an audience as Dire Straits for the first time since Luxembourg on 6
July 1981. Since then they have changed drummers and added
another keyboard player. It's almost a new band, but no one would
guess it from the show that follows; the reward for the long hours put
in at the Wood Wharf.

By comparison with what will come later, it's not a great gig. That
indefinable quality of excitement that binds performer to audience
is missing. Nothing is pushed to the limit; the musicians take their
time to loosen up, feeling their way along without the certainty that
what they're doing is absolutely right.

Backstage after the show the dressing-room doors remain closed
to all outsiders for a long time as every detail is analysed,
suggestions for improvement discussed, faults rectified. Tomorrow
they board the bus. The British tour, the world tour, starts in earnest.

The rock 'n' roll tour has become legend, synonymous with the
kind of debauchery unknown since Nero threw away his fiddle. Just
everyone knows that it's a non-stop whirl of sex, drugs and drink,
groupies queuing for orgies, cocaine piled high on tabletops, hotel
bars drunk dry and trashed.

The reality, as usual, is much more mundane. Few people have the stamina for round-the-clock excess, and those that did are dead long before their time. It's a destiny that's not at all appealing to anyone in Dire Straits.

The truth is that touring is immensely boring, though the end result, playing to a live audience, is so exhilarating that nobody in the band complains. It's a succession of long journeys on the bus, meals grabbed at insalubrious greasy spoons, nights spent in soulless hotel rooms. In Britain, the band will play twenty-two nights straight, which drains them physically and emotionally. The schedule permits them little or no time to visit the places they stop at, nor meet anyone outside their own little world. The sequence of hotel-bus-gig-hotel is repeated night after night. Being successful, Dire Straits can make the whole process as comfortable as possible, but it soon becomes tiresome and tiring.

A typical day might start at 9.30, when Paul or Kevin rings round the rooms to rouse the band members, who trickle down to breakfast over the next hour, before congregating in the lobby while hotel bills are settled and luggage is loaded.

Then it's aboard the bus, which never leaves until a head count has established that all of Dire Straits are accounted for – as Paul says, as long as you have the band there, you can always do the show. The word 'bus' is in fact a misnomer: it's a luxury coach specially adapted for small parties, with more comfortable seats, two folding beds, a sink, a toilet, a fridge, and a video recorder. Many motorway miles are killed watching movies.

Divorced from instruments, equipment and the trappings of music in these surroundings, Dire Straits don't look much like the popular image of a rock 'n' roll band, all flash glamour and excitement. Off-stage nothing distinguishes them, in looks or dress, from any other six people of their age. Nobody would tap them on the shoulder at an identification parade and say: 'These are the musicians, Officer.'

They have wives and children, or steady girlfriends. They live in houses and flats, not mansions or penthouses. They drive mass-produced cars, not Rolls-Royces with personalized plates. Collectively or individually they own no yachts, do not attend sales of Post-Impressionist art at Sotheby's, and avoid fashionable nightspots. They employ neither couturiers to give their private fantasies a public face, nor Press agents to make their private lives public knowledge.

And yet between them, Dire Straits have generated enough money to buy a small Central American state; daily, on this tour, sales figures arrive for *Love Over Gold* that suggest a down payment on a prosperous European republic would be within their price bracket.

Dire Straits, like most musicians, don't do it for the money, and they've managed to retain their personalities on their journey through the looking-glass by eschewing all the trappings of fame and fortune. They have no use for a jet-set lifestyle, false friends or professional hangers-on who bask in their reflected fame.

Nobody in the band considers himself better or more important than anyone else in the world: it's merely the music they create together that sets them apart. They're like actors, each with a specific role to play in the music-making process. That process combines all six into a single unit, yet each has a separate and distinct character off-stage.

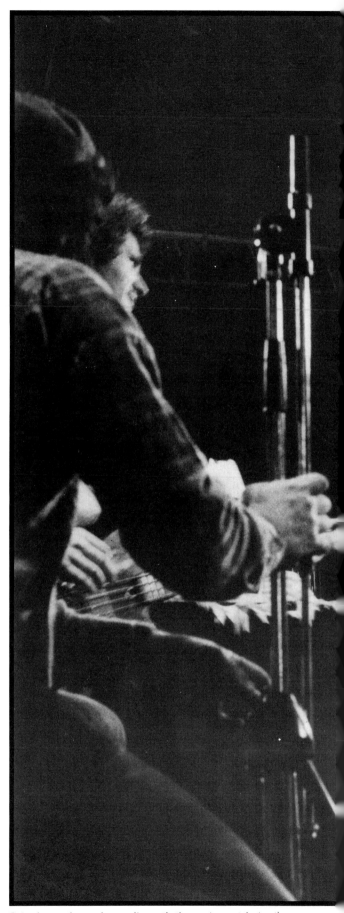

Going home: the road crew dismantle the equipment during the closing notes of the *Local Hero* theme

Nobody could ever mistake Mark Knopfler for anything but the creative force in the band. He spends long hours in the bus staring out of the window, lost in thought. He looks the part, too, giving the impression (though it's not really accurate) of an artist starving in a Paris garret. Financially, of course, nothing could be further from the truth, but his principal luxury, now, is the time to devote himself almost entirely to music.

Inevitably, though, the total picture is more complex. To start with, for a so-called Serious Artist, he spends a lot of time not being serious at all. His face splits readily into an infectious grin as he tells some anecdote from the past, the punchline followed by a great throaty laugh. When he's being cross-examined about the complex emotional impulses behind his songs, the image changes dramatically to that of moody introvert. He refuses to give pat answers – disconcerting journalists used to glib explanations.

He and John Illsley are the sole survivors of the original Dire Straits, and that's no coincidence. Mark takes care of the music, John takes care of business, and there's no competition between them. John has the managing director's kind of interest in the band's career, justly proud of its success and capable of reciting the facts and figures to prove it. Sound and level-headed, he's trusted by Mark to give a clear and decisive opinion whenever he himself is unsure. Whilst Mark often has his head in the clouds, John has his feet firmly on the ground.

Hal Lindes looks too good to be true. His golden hair, laid-back Californian accent and movie-star good looks earmark him as the band's pin-up boy. But he's no ringer put in for the benefit of attracting girls to concerts. Hal's a solid musician with a rapacious thirst for knowledge, ever seeking Mark's advice. On the road he's always at a high level of excitement. Every night is like his first gig, and that enthusiasm whips up the whole band. There's never any danger of the thrill going out of playing music as long as Hal's around.

Alan Clark, Terry Williams and Tommy Mandel are the professional musicians, in the business since childhood. Alan speaks in a soft Geordie accent and is rarely seen without a keyboard to hand. For the tour he's brought along a selection of portable instruments, and sits there playing to himself until someone coaxes him into taking off the headphones and entertaining the bus with a disco version of the nauseous muzak Christmas carols that pursue the band from hotel lobby to motorway café. At times he can also be seen supplementing his yoga exercises with impossible acrobatic feats while hanging from the roof straps.

Fitness is a special problem for Terry on this tour. For several days he was in agony with a pulled muscle in his shoulder and had to be whisked away to hospital for a pain-killing shot before a show at Birmingham National Exhibition Centre. But for him the show always goes on, and afterwards, drink in hand, he entertains with anecdotes drawn from his years in rock 'n' roll, spinning out tales in his lilting Welsh accent. If he had his own TV chat show, Terry wouldn't need guests.

Tommy, too, has years of touring behind him. Like Alan, he never wants to be far from a keyboard, but his enthusiasm borders more closely on eccentricity. One night, for instance, back at the hotel while everyone was having a drink at the bar, Tommy went off to play the piano in a deserted lounge at midnight. He combines activities like this with an endless capacity for unintentionally hilarious remarks that keep the band in stitches while he gazes on in bemused wonder.

Together they make up a happy band without the personal clashes, sulks, arguments and fights that can plague touring groups who are forced to live and work in close proximity. They while away the tedious hours of waiting and travelling by watching movies, reading, chatting, dozing, thinking, and sometimes having an impromptu sing-song. Hal and John take out their acoustic guitars, Alan his keyboards, and the whole bus joins in on vocals, the songbook drawn from early Beatles, Stones, the Everlys – everything but Dire Straits.

Journey's end means being unloaded, either at the hotel to check in, unpack and perhaps make quick phone calls to wives or girlfriends, or at the gig, going straight into the sound check for the night's show.

Afterwards, the band go down into the auditorium to sign autographs for fans, weaving through the equipment piled high for loading on to the two trucks that will take it on to the next gig.

Back at the hotel there's a chance to unwind before an early night. By this time 'early' probably means one o'clock. The whole process starts again at nine-thirty in the morning. It's a perpetual motion machine, locked into the same inexorable sequence of events. But who, or what, started it rolling?

Merry Christmas everybody – and a cup of tea for the band, served on-stage at Wembley by the tour cook, Lorraine Taylor

CHAPTER 2

Nothing but a
House Party

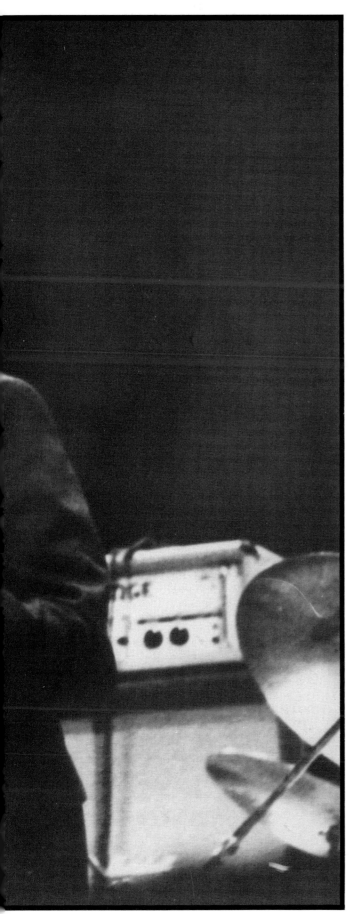

The party begins: the first major London gig, at The Roundhouse, January 1978

The Dire Straits story really starts with a flat in an unimposing twenties mansion block. Now, at the beginning of 1977, the building looks bruised and beaten after half a century doing battle with the elements. Farrar House is no particular landmark. It merges into the background of Deptford, South-East London, to the visitor a fairly anonymous working-class district that had its heyday when the city's dockland was thriving.

This block had already been condemned by the local council as unfit for family accommodation, but in the early seventies an impoverished and enterprising student cajoled the council into renting him a flat there. Others followed, and within a few years students, musicians, artists and writers filled the estate.

John Illsley, a sometime musician and a student at Goldsmiths' College, moved into this community, renting a ground-floor flat with four small bedrooms, a lounge, kitchen and bathroom. It was in a fairly dilapidated condition, but a summer's work with a brush and pot of white paint made it more homely.

John's path to Deptford was paved by the same restlessness that was later to bring Mark Knopfler to the flat. Born in June 1949, the youngest of three brothers, John turned to music at school as an alternative to the regimentation of home and academic life. While at Bromsgrove, a public school in Worcestershire, he started playing acoustic guitar. 'My brother William showed me E, A, and B seventh,' he recalls. 'I had the basic blues chords and I learnt everything else myself. I got a chord book and sheet music and copied all the songs that were happening at that time and got fluent on the guitar.'

The next stage was to join a band, and that's when the problems began. The school group, the Knott, which also featured William, already had three guitarists and a drummer. 'So I said: "I'll play the bass". I took the two top strings off my guitar, the E and the D, and played it with a pick-up on.' It wasn't until six months later that he bought his first proper bass guitar.

By this time, music had become all-consuming. So much so that academic work was put to one side, and there were inevitable confrontations with authority. 'There were some incredible letters that used to go back and forth between my father and my housemaster at school. The housemaster didn't know what a guitar was, so he called it a banjo, and he would write things like: "John doesn't do anything else but play this blasted banjo all day".

'Every week he'd confiscate it, for playing it at the wrong time. It was okay if you played the piano, or if you played the tuba, but if you played the guitar you were associated with the Rolling Stones, who were really anti-Establishment at the time. You were seen as wanting to be like them, which was bad news. So it was really tough at the beginning to get to play at all, because there were so many places, especially at school, where it was really discouraged. I think that helped me. It got like a little battle and I really became very single-minded about it. It cemented in my mind that this was the way I really wanted to channel my energy and creativity.'

Despite adversity, the Knott teetered on. They played in front of the school before the Saturday film show, at other local schools and occasionally fixed up outside gigs. 'We did a village hall, and a rugger club, where they just put a whole load of chipboard down on top of the bath and that was the stage. We actually played in the bathroom; it was a great sound.'

The repertoire was entirely made up of covers, usually of current hits such as the Cream's 'NSU' and 'Spoonful', The Who's 'Anyway, Anyhow, Anywhere', and the old rocker 'Lawdy Miss Clawdy'. John did most of the lead vocals, 'because nobody else could be bothered to learn the bloody words.' Equipment was pretty basic, too: a tiny thirty-watt PA, a few linear amps, and instruments either owned or borrowed. But it was fun and it lasted until the members started leaving school.

'We talked about doing it professionally, maybe getting on a cruise ship or that sort of thing, because there weren't that many gigs around at the time. This was 'sixty-six or 'sixty-seven. We didn't have any idea of what to do or how to go about it. I was up for getting it going, but one guy went off to work for his dad and we just drifted apart. That was the end of it.'

The musical interest had, however, taken its toll of studies, and John found himself with eight O-Levels and an art A-Level – not enough for university or a professional career. So he went to a college of further education near Kettering to try and get English and Physics A-Levels. After the monastic life of Bromsgrove, it was a success socially, but a disaster academically. 'I used to go and play snooker all day, or hang out at the Wimpy Bar.'

And, inevitably, music came back into the picture. 'I started playing in a blues band. There was a really good drummer, me on bass, and a guitarist who used to play in the style of Eric Clapton. He was really good – had a Strat, which was very impressive. We used to play in colleges, the odd pub here or there, supporting local bands for not much money.

'That was a pretty good band. It was based on Cream and we did those sort of numbers. This guitar player used to solo for, like, twenty minutes. We must have had a name, but I think we changed it every time we went out because if it was a bad gig we didn't want them to say: "We won't have them back".'

After a year, John returned home to Leicester, without a job, and to the inevitable round of family arguments. 'My mother kept saying to me: "I think you should go into a bank," because that's what my dad did. I was going for interviews everywhere.'

One attempt to get on the Marks & Spencer's management training course failed at the final interview when he was rude to the managing director; a few weeks with Lloyd's Bank in Rugby was sheer hell. Eventually John came down to London on the recommendation of a friend's father, to take up a job as management trainee for a timber firm. 'And that was fine. I was away from home, I was twenty years old, I'd got my own flat, my own little Ford Popular and I was independent.'

At first it was lonely living out at Woolwich with only a couple of vague acquaintances on the other side of town. But things came together – a girlfriend, a house, a mortgage and hints of a job on the board in a few years' time.

'And then I just got this brainstorm. At the age of twenty-four I said to myself: Look, this is ridiculous. Do I really want to do this for the rest of my life? And I just had to say no.'

He chose to go to Goldsmiths' College to study sociology, paying his way by working part-time on an account for the timber firm. 'I really enjoyed it; for the first time I was interested in academic work.

A guitar hero is born: Mark at an early London club gig

I stuck with it, but of course your frame of mind tends to change once you're in that sort of world again, and I started to think seriously about music. I started playing the guitar a bit more and I met some guys at college who wanted to muck about a bit, and we got an atrocious band together. I was getting interested in playing music again and I thought to myself, I'm really keen on doing this. I didn't have any idea of how it was going to work out.'

Meanwhile, John and his girlfriend opened a record shop in North London, which gradually began to lose money and had to be abandoned. So did the relationship, and John moved out, and into 1 Farrar House.

He wasn't alone for long. 'I was talking with some friends of mine in the pub and one of them worked with Dave Knopfler as a social worker on Greenwich Council. She said that he'd just been thrown out of his flat or something and needed somewhere to live. He came round and we got on well, so he moved in.'

Dave, too, was a guitarist, and he and John used to sit around the flat and strum away together. At the time, John was in a band called Blind Alley: 'It did one gig and that was it, the band was so appalling.'

Dave had talked about his guitarist brother, and the day soon came when Mark and John were to meet at the flat. 'I'd been out all night and came in about ten in the morning. I walked into the kitchen, started making myself a cup of tea, walked into the lounge and there was this guy lying on the floor with his head propped up against a chair. He was fast asleep, fully clothed in denim with leather boots. He had a guitar slouched over his waist. I thought, Fuck me, this must be Mark.

'Of course he woke up then and we started chatting away. We got along well immediately. And from that day on we seemed to spend an awful lot of time together, going up to the West End, out to pubs and clubs, just generally hanging out.'

The Knopfler brothers' lives up to this point had had the same threads of music and restlessness as John's. Mark was born in August 1949, David three-and-a-half years later, the sons of a Hungarian Jewish Communist architect who had fled the Nazis to England in 1939. He settled in Glasgow, married a teacher and left the Communist Party. Dave takes up the story: 'We were born in Glasgow and moved to Newcastle when I was four or five. Being a leftie, my father worked for the local authority – he wouldn't go into private practice. I don't think he really carved out a career for himself; I think he got screwed by the corruption in the North-East. My dad was basically the straight man, freaking out about it and making a fuss.'

By a strange coincidence, Pete Murdoch, who was Dire Straits' first roadie and later became crew foreman, lived in the same Glasgow street as the Knopflers, though nobody found out until they'd been working together for a year. Dave recalls: 'We were too small to see over the fence, but Pete and I used to chuck toy bricks at each other. I remember thinking that when I chucked my bricks I wished I hadn't because his weren't as good as mine.'

When they moved to Newcastle, the Knopfler parents encouraged an interest in music. Mark says: 'I remember my mum playing the piano – she still does a little. My dad could play the violin a bit, but I only saw him playing it once. They both had musical ears, digged music.'

School for both was Gosforth Grammar, and there, too, Dave

remembers the traditional hostility to modern music that gave an allure to rock 'n' roll: 'I'm sure school had a lot to do with it, a reaction against, rather than positive – for me, anyway. I remember being kicked off the piano, and kicked out of school endlessly . . . put on detention for playing piano, stuff like that. The music classes were strictly classical, and I remember being kicked out and told that I was wasting everybody's time. I think something similar happened to Mark with the same teacher. That was because we wouldn't be disciplined into reading music. I mean, I'd go away and cheat really, play it by ear and then come back and pretend to be reading it.'

On their trips into town, the brothers would press their noses up against the two guitar shops. An early dream was a salmon-pink Fender, Hank Marvin style, costing £168. But when the first guitar came, ambitions had to be scaled down to a Hofner Super Solid with two pick-ups. Dave still has it at home.

'On the hand-me-down principle, I wound up with it. My dad first bought it for Mark. It was quite a big deal because Mark turned down a school holiday – he could have gone on a cruise for ten days or something – but he said: "No, I'd rather have a guitar." Of course, we never had an amp.

'I used to play the Hofner whenever Mark wasn't around: "House Of The Rising Sun", stuff like that. I bought myself an acoustic guitar for ten shillings, like a Tommy Steele job. I think Mark taught me a little. We must have played together a bit, but I don't think it was any big deal. I think I would occasionally tie him down to showing me something.'

Mark would put bands together for school dances, hanging out with those who were playing music. Dave got together with a few friends and formed a group called Rock Machine in which he played drums.

'To call it a band is too much. I think we did two gigs. Mark wasn't in it – it would have been a different story if he had been. I don't think either of us were the archetypal kids who were living and dying for it, playing the working men's clubs, making a living from it and going to school. We played in bands and cared about it, but I'm sure a lot of kids from there became journalists, teachers, whatever, and that was the end of it.'

Mark did take one small step into the professional world of music when he linked up with a schoolfriend, Sue Hercombe, in an acoustic guitar/vocal duo, and they played a couple of times on a local TV magazine programme.

'We were doing fingerstyle and harmony singing. We did everything from Incredible String Band to Bob Dylan. We were just two young kids. She was about fifteen and I was sixteen.'

His interest in music covered many styles. Early heroes included Ricky Nelson's guitarist, James Burton, and Elvis Presley's guitar man, Scotty Moore, as well as blues players like Lonnie Johnson.

'But I never sat down with a record player and tried to copy licks note for note. It's something I always tried to avoid, really. I'd try to pick up on the feeling, though. I remember the first time I heard B.B. King, when I was sixteen or something, at school. It was the *Live At The Regal* album. That made a big impression on me. The audience response and the feel of the guitar-playing, you know? It's never been academic for me.'

Around this time, Mark did get to make a record. Dave: 'Some guy who was a market gardener, I think, paid for Mark to go to London to

make a demo disc. They went into a proper studio and cut it in half an hour, or an hour. It was never released. I don't think anybody ever did anything with it, either, it was just made. It was never intended to be of master quality, it was a demo.

'It was a real good song, called "Summer's Coming My Way", very good for its time. For what it was and for what he had available to him it was a real brave effort. He was still really in the folk clubs at the time.'

Mark's adolescence in Newcastle was something he was later to turn back to time and again in songs, particularly on the first album. For example, Dave recalls the background to 'Down To The Waterline': 'Mark got a gig with the National Youth Theatre or something like that. It was quite a big deal, anyway. He got a part in one of those sixties things, like *Julius Caesar* in black polo-neck jumpers and machine-guns. Experimental theatre, they called it then, and it was still relatively new. This was when Mark was about fourteen or fifteen.

'He told me about coming back on the train every night and seeing the river and the lights. I remember one night him being quite blown away by all these lights, and he did a painting of the River Tyne which my parents have still got on the wall. The imagery in "Down To The Waterline" comes from walking along the Tyne at night with his girl.'

Another early impression was made by the Spanish City, a fairground at Whitley Bay, later to become the background for 'Tunnel Of Love'.

Dave goes on: 'I used to leave primary school, get on a train without paying, go to Whitley Bay, which is about eight miles, hide in the toilet until the ticket inspector had gone, jump off at the other

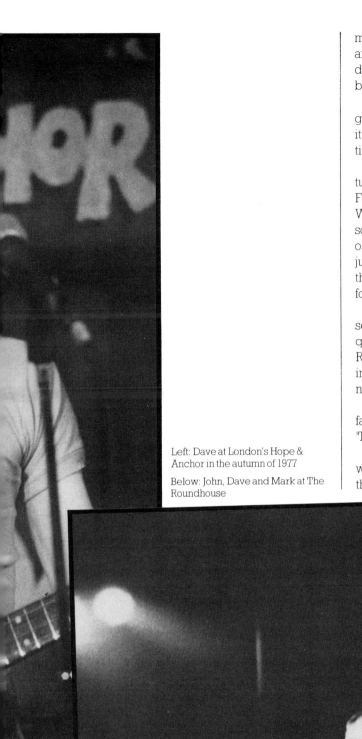

Left: Dave at London's Hope & Anchor in the autumn of 1977

Below: John, Dave and Mark at The Roundhouse

end, walk down about three-quarters of a mile to the Spanish City and spend several hours playing fruit machines. I knew all the wheezes on fruit machines, figuring out ways to get enough money to pay for rides. I was obsessed with fairgrounds; Mark and I used to go to them together quite a lot.'

The brothers were parted in 1967, when Mark headed south to spend a year studying journalism at Harlow Technical College. A guitar came too, naturally, for informal sessions at parties and, in the summer, on the grass outside with other students. There were field trips, too, to check out bands at a nearby blues club in Bishops Stortford, and sometimes up in London.

Course over, Mark went up to Leeds, where he worked as a reporter on the *Yorkshire Evening Post* for two years before deciding that the shorthand notebook and battered typewriter were not for him, and he went to the city's university to take an English degree. There were bands here, too, but nothing serious until his studies were completed. Meanwhile, Mark had got married in Leeds, but it was not to last.

'The first day that I left university I said, right, I'm off to London to play in a rock band – and I went off. I just opened *Melody Maker* and looked for the biggest ad. I got off the train, went along, and there were other guitarists coming out of the audition who said good luck. I went in and got the gig.'

The band was Brewer's Droop. As the name and the title of one of their most popular numbers, 'Beer', suggest, they were not to be taken too seriously. Based around High Wycombe, they'd been playing around the college circuit for a few years but hadn't risen into the big league. Their philosophy, as explained by leader Ron Watts, was to be 'a real, honest, good-time band, trying to communicate and letting audiences have a ball.'

'I played with them for about two months,' Mark recalls. 'Starved to death. They were playing cajun R'n'B but they'd played basically the same set for three years. There was a fair amount of beer went down. But my marriage was breaking up, the band was breaking up, no money, no nothing. I suppose it was pretty good experience in a way.'

It wasn't put to use immediately, for Mark went off to teachers' training college and then landed a job as a lecturer at Loughton College in Essex.

Dave, meanwhile, had left home and gone to Bristol Polytechnic. 'I was going to take a year off but my mother wasn't having it. She was putting pressure on me to go, so I went, which was pretty handy because I enjoyed it as it turned out. I was playing keyboards with a guy called Pete Ward, who I lost contact with because he failed his first-year exams. I was looking around for bands, but there wasn't anything there for me, not until I got into the folkie thing again, which seemed to be about the only thing you could do if you were a guitarist.'

Dave left college and went to work for the DHSS. Mark had just moved to Loughton and would drive over on his Honda 250 to visit.

Dave: 'I had two guitars. I had my own, a Harmony Sovereign which cost me £40, and this other one I'd picked up in the garbage pile of a flat which I cleaned up and restored. Mark and I used to play on these guitars.'

Eleven months later, Dave packed in his job and moved down to London, staying for a month with Mark in his Buckhurst Hill flat.

The first tour – the Straits were supporting Talking Heads

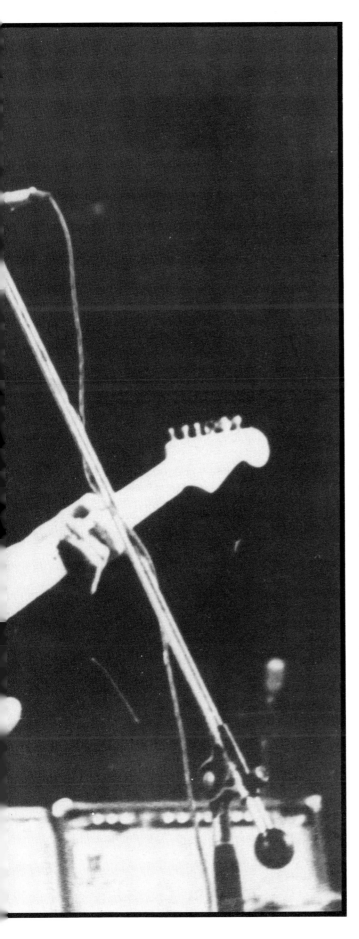

'That was a formative thing, as I recollect it,' says Dave. 'The two of us were in that nasty flat, and going down to the pub, getting the fish and chips or the Chinese takeaway at eleven o'clock, going back, getting out the acoustic guitars and playing till we fell asleep at two o'clock. And that was really the routine, every night.

'A lot of it was the first stages of what was to become the first album. Some of the songs were there in embryo. I remember the melody line of "Lions" in particular. When we were in Basing Street recording the first album, we were stuck for one more song. Mark had to go away and write one, and I remember suggesting to him that he use that melody line, which he did.

'It was more to do with a sound, a style, a feel, a groove, than actual songs. I remember when I found John in Deptford, I phoned Mark after I'd got the flat. I was quite excited about Mark coming down and meeting up with John, because I felt that he was a potential third member of a band.'

Mark, meanwhile, had already formed a band with friends from Loughton College. 'There was a singer and a bass player and a drummer. I used to play guitar and sing harmonies. We did rockabilly, R'n'B. I had this Selmer amplifier which I used to put on two chairs and play.'

This was the Café Racers, a band with a floating personnel which built up a solid reputation on the London college/pub circuit. They were particular favourites at the King's Head in Islington, packing it out and spilling out on to the pavements in the summer of 1976. There were no original songs, though, just old gold like 'Good Morning Little Schoolgirl', 'Move It', Jerry Lee Lewis classics.

'We even did a version of "Not Fade Away". I used to use a wah-wah pedal on it, just like James Burton did when he played with the Everly Brothers. It was a real good version. We did a couple of Everlys things like that; I think we even did "Bird Dog". I was playing a Gibson Les Paul Special which plugged straight into the amp. I used to have to use a pick [plectrum] a lot more then; it was a combination of lead and rhythm playing.'

When the band were short of a bassist one night, John was invited to sit in. The combination worked and he played a couple more gigs. But the band was going nowhere, and both John and Mark knew it.

John: 'There was no big deal about it at all. But I do remember distinctly, one night after we had finished rehearsing, Mark and I went to a pub close by and we were talking about his songs. He wanted a vehicle to do his own material, so I said, "Let's get something together and do it ourselves, then".'

In April 1977, Mark packed in his flat and moved in with John and Dave at Farrar House, though he still kept his job at Loughton for a few more months. 'I enjoyed two years of teaching, but the third year I thought to myself, Oh God, I just can't do this for the rest of my life, I just can't. The songs were pushing very hard.'

Through hours of practice and rehearsal, the songs emerged, and it quickly became obvious to John that not only was Mark a talented guitarist, but a gifted songwriter too. 'He was exciting, a really different guitar player. I'd played with a lot, and he was exceptional. He used to play with a plectrum in the Racers, rather than the finger-picking style he uses now in Dire Straits. I should think that the finger-picking style was something he used to do at home for hours and hours – when he couldn't find a plectrum, knowing him.

'He didn't used to talk much about the songs. He just used to say; "I think I've written a good one," and that was it. I'd say, I'd like to hear it and then he'd play it. We used to have a lot of conversations at that time and I think that we were pretty stimulating for each other, and that might have helped with the songs. It was almost as if he tripped a wire and started to write.'

Through the spring and early summer of 1977 the songs kept coming. 'Wild West End' was written about Mark's wanderings around London; 'Southbound Again' came from memories of trips to the capital. Of 'Sultans of Swing', Mark says: '"Sultans" was written quite a long time before the band; I hadn't met John then. Dave was living somewhere down in Greenwich and we just went out to the pub – I think it was called the Swan, something like that, in Greenwich High Road – and had a game of pool and a couple of pints. There was a jazz band playing, and there was nobody in there except us and a couple of kids in the corner.

'They did a couple of requests. I asked them for "Creole Love Call", and it was great. There are loads of bands like that. They're postmen, milkmen, accountants, draughtsmen, teachers. They just get together Sunday lunchtimes, night-times, and they play trad. And it's funny because they play this New Orleans music note for note – in Greenwich.'

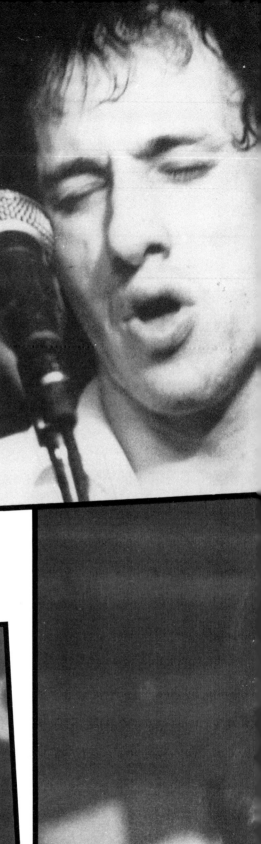

John remembers that originally 'Sultans' was very different. The lyrics were the same but the tune was completely different. 'I have the feeling that he wrote some music one day and said, Hey, I've got some great new chords for "Sultans"!'

'In The Gallery' was inspired by a visit made by John and Mark to a modern art gallery owned by a friend of Mark's in Shaftesbury Avenue. John says: 'We were wandering around and neither of us could believe the shit that was there. It was garbage; there's no other word for it. As far as we were concerned, it shouldn't even have been considered in the same breath as Art.

'On the way back, Mark sat in the back of the car and he was furiously writing. I didn't say anything, and we drove back to Deptford in complete silence. I got out of the car and asked him if he was coming in and he said: "I've just got to finish something off." He came in about an hour and a half later, and he'd written this song.

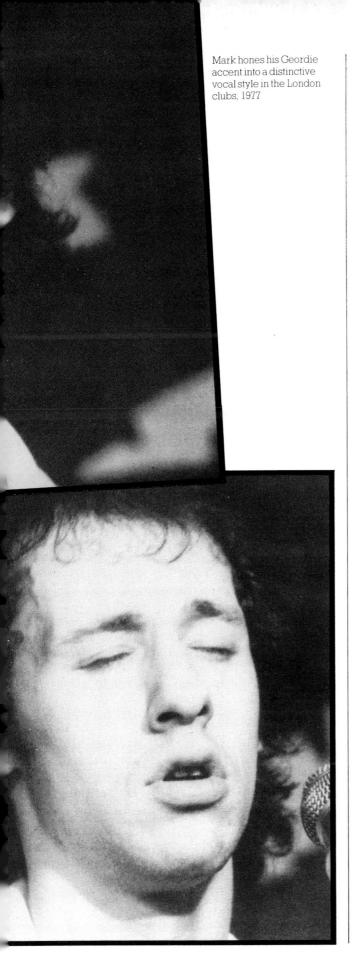

Mark hones his Geordie accent into a distinctive vocal style in the London clubs, 1977

'For a while, he didn't have the music for it, but when we were jamming in the flat we had the lick, which we just used to muck around with. We were sitting there one day and it was suddenly: "Hey these two go together!" Things like that happened occasionally, which was fun. We used to finish off songs in the band. We used to throw ideas out, or throw ideas in, whatever.'

With songs taking shape, two guitarists and a bassist, the next stage was to find a drummer. 'Mark just said one day: "I know this drummer and he's a very sensitive player. I think he'll fit in." Pick came down and it was the most natural thing.'

In terms of experience, Pick Withers was worlds apart from the other three. An early memory for him is seeing the Boys' Brigade band marching down the street to the beat of a big bass drum. 'For some reason I wanted to get that drum. I had to go through a lot of red tape – be in the Boys' Brigade for a year, then play the bugle for a year. My great piece was playing "The Last Post" at camp. Then I had to wait for a vacancy and I finally got this drum. I used to drive my parents mad.'

At seventeen, he became a professional musician and joined a band called the Primitives. For three years he kept the beat on tour in Italy, playing a collection of R'n'B oldies and weak band originals. On returning to England, there was a dizzying sequence of sessions and a band called Spring, who recorded an album for RCA without much commercial or critical success. 'The critics thought it was pretentious, and in retrospect, it was.'

He then moved to Dave Edmunds' Rockfield Studios in South Wales, to a not particularly lucrative job as house drummer: 'You'd have to ask for forty pence for fags.' However, it did give Pick an opportunity to work with an impressively varied collection of artists, among them Bert Jansch, Howard Werth, Michael Chapman and Del Shannon.

He met up with Mark at the house of a mutual friend, where, Mark claims, 'He was busy starving to death.' When Pick came down to Farrar House, the effect was immediately obvious to all. John says: 'For me, as a bass player, to be playing with Pick Withers was fantastic for a start. I'd never played with anybody as good as him.

'I really felt very shy, initially, about playing. He used to play in a folk club and he was very delicate – nowhere near how he ended up, thrashing the kit, as he put it. A great player, then, and I think he became a better player over the years, though he'd probably dispute that. He certainly didn't like some of the aspects of rock'n'roll, the fact that it had to be four to the bar. He didn't like to do straightforward drumming too much.'

There was now a proper band, the personnel set for intensive rehearsals. John remembers 'spending hours playing at that time, in this tiny little bedroom at the flat. There was just enough room for a drum kit and three guys to stand up, and that was it. I tried to soundproof it, I put up a false ceiling and filled it with sound insulation material. We had carpets all over the walls.

'It was a horrible den, stinking. With everybody smoking all the time, after twenty minutes you couldn't see across the room. I just remember playing and playing, all the time, every day, for hours. And suddenly we realized that we had a certain style. The way we played was very thin, but everything was in its place, even though it was incredibly basic.'

And finally the confidence came to take the music to an audience.

CHAPTER 3
Spit and Polish

Summer 1977 was a great time to start up a band – provided you were under twenty, couldn't sing, couldn't play, couldn't write songs and wanted to revel in amateurism. Britain was undergoing its most profound change in popular music for a decade. Hundreds of bands were springing up around the country in rebellion against the slick soullessness of the professionals who had come to dominate the music scene.

The rock 'n' roll dream of the spotty kid standing nervously up on a stage to deliver his songs had been shattered. By the mid-seventies, 'rock star' had come to mean a twenty-seven-year-old university graduate with three years of conservatory training behind him, buried beneath a mountain of keyboards and playing a three-part suite about pixies on Mars.

'Rock' became synonymous with albums, preferably three-LP concepts with grandiose themes, music pinched from the classics and lyrics suitable for stuffing pillow cases. Pomposity bred smug self-satisfaction and an inflated view of the musician's role. Fans waited years for the latest *Meisterwerk* to be shaped, crafted and finely tuned in studios bristling with time-wasting technology, conveniently close to exotic, palm-fringed beaches.

'Superstars' spent most of their time touring America in luxury superjets, stopping off to play in front of tens of thousands in football stadiums for which they were paid colossal sums of money. Their chief hobby was throwing television sets out of hotel windows.

Britain represented slim pickings and thus was rarely visited. The duration of such tours as there were was determined by Inland Revenue rules regarding residence for tax purposes. The supergroups played long seasons at huge venues in an atmosphere of cathedral-like solemnity. Audiences sat quietly in their seats, were ordered not to applaud during numbers, listened to interminable solos and watched apocalyptic light shows.

This was hardly rock 'n' roll.

The singles chart was run for the benefit of radio stations, a dumping-ground for sentimental ballads, over-produced prototypes for concept albums, and teenybop dreck for the pre-teens.

Effectively, popular music had been cut off from its roots; working-class kids had been muscled out. No longer the outlet for frustration and anger, it had become part of the Establishment. The first rumblings of discontent were heard in 1976. By 1977 punk rock was in full cry.

In London, kids were clambering on to stages in grotty little dives for an audience of their peers to spit overpriced lager at them (and lob the can in afterwards if the band was *real* good). Instrumental dexterity was taboo, although a rudimentary knowledge was preferable to avoid serious injury. Songs were faster than the speed of light, chords chattering out repetitively until the band lurched to a halt after a two-minute journey. The tone of the lyrics ranged between hatred and boredom, singers spitting out their rage at society, family, country, everything, in a flat monotone.

It was important to be young and disgusting, to emphasize your disaffection from the grown-up world around you with the ripped rags you wore and the deliberate amateurism and inarticulateness of your music. Crude it may have been, but it brought back feeling and passion to rock 'n' roll. Temporarily, it cut away the army of minders, accountants, jobsworths, tax shelter experts and businessmen that kept superstars isolated from their fans, and gave band and audience equal starring roles in the performance.

The embryonic Dire Straits were caught between the two camps, taking the musicianship from one side and the passion from the other. They wrote and performed well-crafted songs at a time when that kind of music was most definitely out of fashion.

Inevitably, they had to make their live debut at a punk festival. They used the name of Mark's old band, Café Racers – Dave even had T-shirts printed up with the name on – and played on the grassy area at the back of Farrar House in July 1977.

John grins. 'There were about thirty punk bands on that day. They were all walking down the street with bass bins, bass drums, guitars with three strings on – it was the most shambolic bunch of musicians you've ever seen. You wouldn't call most of them musicians, really, they were in it for a laugh.

'They'd get up and start singing "My old man is a cunt" and "I fucking hate my mother" – all completely out of tune. Nobody was clapping, so the band would just stop and say: "We're gonna do a fucking encore now. Are you bastards going to clap? Well, we're gonna do it anyway. *Onetwofreefour*", and another song would come out. The whole thing was hilarious.'

The Racers played for about half an hour, before Squeeze, who were Deptford's biggest band at the time. The set included originals like 'Sultans of Swing', 'Down To The Waterline', 'Southbound Again' and 'In The Gallery', mixed in with a couple of Ry Cooder songs and Brenda Lee's 'Sweet Nothin's'. The delights of 'Wild West End', with Mark on his National Steel guitar, were lost on most of the audience as a strong wind wafted much of the music away.

'It was a great gig, a lot of fun,' Dave remembers.

Their second live appearance was shortly afterwards. And at the Deptford Albany, supporting Squeeze, the band had a new name.

John explains: 'We were throwing names around all the time. A friend of Pick's suggested Dire Straits, mostly as a comment on our financial situation and we all went: "What a great name!" But we were the only ones who thought so. Everybody else thought it was terrible. The first time we met Ed Bicknell he said: "Can you change the name?" and Johnny Stainze at Phonogram said, "Great band. But the name – what we gonna do with that?"'

More gigs followed, but it was a hand-to-mouth existence, especially after Mark quit his job. Work was hard to find, as John, who spent a lot of time hassling for gigs, discovered. 'I'd phone up the Hope & Anchor and people like that and they'd ask whether we were a punk band. When I said no, they'd say: "Sorry, we're only taking punk bands." People weren't interested in a rhythmic rock 'n' roll band playing their own songs. They wanted somebody who was going to come in and spit over everybody.'

The economics of playing London's small club/pub circuit were eating away at savings. A £50 fee would be swallowed by hiring a PA and petrol; a £75 gig would need a bigger PA, at greater cost, and the band might just end up with three or four pounds each a night, which could turn out to be a week's work.

'It was pretty tough for a while, literally paying the rent,' John says. 'I used to do quite a bit of cooking in the flat. I made these big stews and lentil soups, things like that, which would last for a long time.'

An early appearance at a summer party for the *Honky Tonk* radio show, whose presenter, Charlie Gillett, was the first to play the band's demo tape

Mark adds: 'It was touch and go for a bit. We'd given up our jobs just to put it all into the band, thinking, Screw it, this is what we all believe in and this is what we really want to do. So we did. It was a real concerted act of will and there was a lot of drive. John and I would do a lot of motoring around getting things, getting wires, getting amps and speakers fixed, booking our gigs. It was a very good thing that I had John with me then because we could make each other go a little bit harder.'

More valuable savings were pooled to record a demo record at Pathway Studios that summer.

'It's a little eight-track studio up in Islington,' explains Chas Herington, now in charge of Dire Straits' lights. 'I was working there as a house engineer and they booked in one weekend as Café Racers. They did four tracks. Everybody else was doing new wave stuff, and I was doing a lot of Stiff acts – the Damned, Wreckless Eric, people like that.'

The tracks laid down were 'Sultans of Swing' – regarded by those who've heard it as the best recorded version – 'Wild West End', 'Down To The Waterline', and 'Water Of Love', all of which were re-recorded on the first album. They also did, 'Sacred Loving', a song written by Dave which was shortly dropped from the set.

The problem of what to do with the tape was solved when John remembered Charlie Gillett, who he'd called up for advice when he and his former girlfriend were setting up the record shop. Charlie was presenting a show on BBC Radio London, broadcast at midday on Sundays, which had an excellent reputation for playing currently unfashionable but high quality music, including tapes sent in by up-and-coming bands. John dropped off the Straits cassette for an opinion, but so impressed was Charlie that he played it over the air that Sunday without telling the band, who were moving furniture for a friend that day and thus missed the show.

There was an immediate reaction. Several record company A & R men heard the tape and were very impressed. John Stainze of Phonogram was in the shower, walked out and stood by the radio, water dripping off him on to the carpet. Another A & R man, driving out of London, pulled his car into the side of the road because the signal was getting fainter the further he drove. The tape was played again in subsequent weeks, and soon there was a sizeable queue of record company executives wanting to see Dire Straits in action.

Dave remembers the excitement. 'Charlie played that bloody tape to death on the radio. He really did. And he played it with a "Now, stop, listen, this is the most important thing I've got to play you today" kind of attitude. It was like winning the pools – how many bands get that kind of thing? Nowadays, playing a demo tape's no big deal, but then it was really something.

'Charlie did us a hell of a big favour. He was very upset that he didn't get to sign us for his own label, but he was honest enough to admit that he thought a major would be better for us. He could have come down and said: "Look, I'll play your tape on the radio if you sign a deal." But he certainly didn't do anything like that. He was great. It was the best break that any band could ever hope for.'

There was a definite buzz in the air about the band from this moment on. The music Press went along to gigs, though early reviews were mostly taken up with discussing who was the major influence on Mark. The chief contenders were J. J. Cale and Ry Cooder, both guitarists who used a similar spare style, though

Dave at a London pub gig before the Straits were signed to a record deal: 'I remember thinking, this is going down a bit well'

Captain Beefheart, Randy Newman, Lou Reed, Bruce Springsteen, Little Feat and Eric Clapton were thrown in for good measure. The overwhelming opinion was that the band was American in sound and style, which was the complete antithesis of most of the music being played around London at the time.

At night, the amount of work gradually started to pick up. During the day, John and Mark wandered from record company to record company, listening to offers, talking about the future.

John particularly, knew it was a crucial time. 'We wanted to find something out about the record business. When you don't know anything about it and everybody's saying the tape is the best thing since sliced bread, you think, What's happening here? We grew really cautious. At the end of each day we used to sit down and talk the whole thing through until we realized what we wanted. All the deals that were being done then were singles deals, with maybe one album, but we wanted a four or five album deal so the band would have time to develop.'

Record companies were eager to sign Dire Straits – but on their own terms. One offered the band £1,500 to record the first album, which would then be 'thrown against the wall to see if it sticks'. Another plied them with drink and dope in an effort to get them to sign on the dotted line.

Dave remembers seeing one A & R man at a gig at the King's Head in Islington 'with his eyes closed and his head up. He was obviously in some state of financial bliss because he thought he was going to sign us. I remember thinking, this is going down a bit well. But I didn't have the experience to compare it with. I didn't know that to really go down well at a live gig in a rock pub meant a lot. I thought we were good, but you just get acclimatized to making good music; I didn't know whether it would come to anything.'

On the advice of journalist Richard Williams, the band went to see lawyer Robert Allan, who took over negotiations. Finally, they worked out an acceptable deal with Phonogram and were signed in autumn 1977, much to the delight of John Stainze, who had been strongly pressing their case. As a result, Mark got a publishing deal for his songs from Rondor.

Contrary to popular opinion, bands do not become millionaires overnight as soon as they are signed to record companies; in Dire Straits' case, the six-figure sum that was widely quoted at the time just didn't exist. Their deal was, however, a very good one, and unusual for a new band at that time in that it allowed for three albums before Phonogram had an option to drop them.

The band received some money on signing, but most of their advance was spread out to pay for recording the albums – up to £25,000 for each on a non-recoupable basis, that is, without any of the costs up to that amount coming out of the band's royalties. (Subsequently, the contract was re-negotiated, and the first three albums cost over £150,000 to make; the fourth *Love Over Gold,* alone cost around £110,000.)

The pressing need for Dire Straits now was a manager to organize their careers and help them make the step up from pubs and clubs into a touring band. John Stainze contacted Ed Bicknell early in December 1977, to say that Phonogram had signed Dire Straits and that he needed an agent to find them gigs.

Ed was working at the NEMS agency, mainly booking tours for American new wave acts on the Sire label. A one-time drummer, he'd played in a band with John Whetton (now with Asia) which became Mogul Thrash and then turned into the Average White Band – whereupon Ed and John were sacked for not being Scottish. He became an agent and worked his way up through the business, managing a couple of commercially unsuccessful bands, Isotope and the Surprise Sisters, along the way.

His career was at a low when John's call came through. 'I was thinking of giving up the music business. I'd just done a tour with Richard Hell and the Void-Oids that had completely finished me off. They were the worst group I'd ever been involved with.'

Ed went round to Phonogram's offices, heard the Charlie Gillett tape and was immediately impressed. He was invited out to dinner – 'the cheapest Greek meal I think I've ever had in my life' – and taken to Dingwalls, the club in North London. As they walked in, Dire Straits were already into their opening number, 'Down To The Waterline'.

'The first thing I noticed was that it wasn't necessary to stand at the back of the room; they were very quiet. I'd just done the Ramones, who were deafening. You just soaked up the music when you walked in – you could actually walk right up to the front without being blasted through the back.

'The second thing I noticed was that Mark was playing a red Stratocaster, which immediately made me think of Hank Marvin, who I had idolized in the sixties. And I was sort of drawn into the songs. What they were playing was what subsequently became the first LP, plus shuffle numbers. They were essentially doing very American-sounding shuffle music in a way, things like "Eastbound Train", "Southbound Again" and their jazzed-up version of Chuck Berry's "Nadine".

'By the second or third number I went over to Stainze and said: "I'd like to manage this band, they're great. Tell you what, John, I'll give you five per cent of everything that I make – get me this group!" And he said: "Fuck me, Ed, that's not necessary!" I was so excited about it – I didn't know how to go about getting them. The set finished and Stainze took me into the cupboard that served as a dressing-room. As I went in, I fell over the red Strat and knocked it on to the floor. And they all looked up at me as if to say: "What's the dog dragged in?"'

John agrees. 'He had this coat with a big fur collar, and silver hair. I thought he was a right flash prat.'

The next day, Mark, John and Dave went round to Ed's office, which had been hurriedly transformed into a hive of activity suitable for a big-shot manager.

'I got my secretary to make the phone ring all the time, as if I was getting loads of calls, and I would snatch the phone up and say: "Take the fuck off! Five thousand pounds!" They sat on this little plastic banquette, amazed by all this.'

Ed was currently booking a British tour with Talking Heads, and he offered the Straits a support slot. He thrust copies of the Heads' 77 album into their hands, and the three musicians went away to consider the offer. Dave was reluctant; Mark and John thought Ed was completely mad, but that he appeared to know what he was doing. They called up the next day and agreed; the wheels were set in motion.

'The thing I told them that they should never do, which I've subsequently heard is the reason I got them, is that they should

John on the first British tour

never sign an agency contract with anybody, let alone NEMS. This really impressed them, apparently. It was possible for me to manage Dire Straits while still working at NEMS from December 1977 till February 1979, when I left, with virtually nobody there being aware of the fact. And I used their time, their phones, their telex, their secretaries.

'It often happens that people in agencies end up managing artists, either because they have no manager or because the manager they have got is useless. I mean, of the managers we were dealing with there, I would say a good seventy-five percent were absolutely incompetent, so you just ended up covering for them all the time. For instance, at that particular point, none of the Sire acts had got management. My one regret about the Straits' success was that I lost Talking Heads, because I didn't have the time.'

The tour with the Heads started on 20 January 1978: the Straits were paid £50 a night for a fifty minute set. Both bands stayed in the same hotels, travelled in the same van and used the same equipment. It wasn't a life of luxury, but was definitely several notches up the scale for the Straits. And it was a lot of fun.

John is enthusiastic. 'The Heads were really great to work with. We used to get sound checks, which are almost unheard of for support bands. We got encores every night and really went down well. We were playing medium-sized gigs, nothing huge; a university with a thousand people was top whack, I think.'

Ed agrees: 'It was a very happy tour. The bands have played together subsequently at festivals and they're great friends. I think the Straits were a bit bemused by the fact that Tina Weymouth had never changed her bass strings, ever. The Heads saw the Straits changing guitar strings one night, and I think David Byrne or Jerry Harrison asked them why they did it. Upon examining the Heads' guitars they found all these rusty strings, because they didn't clean them either. Afterwards, the Heads started buying strings and cleaning their guitars.'

As he was dealing with both bands, Ed went along on the tour and had an opportunity to get to know his new charges.

'I liked all of them that day I met them, but it was soon very apparent that they each had their little box. Mark always came over as being a bit *strange,* mainly because of his manner of speaking, which is between long pauses. He had a very stilted way of expressing himself, so you were never quite sure of what was going on in his head, or whether he meant something else. You would be talking, and he would suddenly drop something in that had nothing to do with what you were discussing.

'David was suffering even then from the younger brother syndrome. This manifested itself in him moaning all the time – I think because he couldn't make a big impact musically in the context of where he was at the time. And this continued for his entire time in the group, only it revved up. As we got more and more successful, his moaning got worse and worse. But even then he would moan about the monitors, or the amps, or the fact that Chris and Tina were sitting near the heater in the van. He didn't like the hotel, or whatever.

'John was always very level-headed, ran everything. He knows exactly the business side of the group. He might not be the Jaco Pastorius of rock, but he's made a huge contribution. He's almost like a centrifugal point around which everyone revolves, because they know that he will take the sensible attitude to everything. He understands money and things like that – he was doing the accounts, for instance, on bits of paper with a pencil. He's probably the closest to me, personality-wise, I can ring him up and discuss a VAT return with him, which Mark wouldn't be interested in – and there's no reason why he should be, of course.

'But it's very useful to have one person in the operation who they all trust. I mean, they all trust me, but he's on their side of the camp – he knows that I'm not stealing money off them, or that Joe Bloggs the promoter isn't.

'Pick was a mystery – still is, in a way. Pick's experience of groups had consisted of spells with people like Dave Edmunds, playing "Sabre Dance" faster and faster, and Bert Jansch and Ralph McTell and all that sort of thing. I think Pick probably looked back on his formative musical years rather more fondly than they deserved. He's glamorized them in his mind. I think one of the reasons he's now moved back near Rockfield is because that was one of the happy periods in his life. But he was probably in misery, living on cans of cold beans and getting five quid a week on Bert Jansch sessions.

'He was always a little out of the other four. Apart from anything else, John, David and Mark were all living in the same house. Pick came into the band last, he was older than the others, and he'd had more band experience. I think he'd been a bit embittered by things that had happened to him. Anyway, he was outside the other three and as the years went by that became more and more obvious. Like, he would rarely attend meetings, would rarely express any joy or enthusiasm about anything. With the others, there's a genuine interest in the way their career's going and what's happened to the music they're creating. Pick never really had that.

'The band was structured very democratically, which in fact doesn't work. In some bands, the reason why the bass player gets his appalling song on side two is because it's democratic. It doesn't work that way. I suppose in a sense it was more democratic musically than it is now, but then the music was a lot simpler.'

John says: 'I think it was always in the back of my mind that the band would always be a vehicle for Mark's songs. That's the way it started, that's the way it developed, and presumably that's the way it will go on until something else happens. I don't mind that. I think one of the reasons that bands become successful, and stay successful, is that there's something that people can identify with. I think it's very confusing sometimes if you have a supposedly democratic band where everybody does his own song. For the majority of people, their interest in rock music is peripheral, really, so they need a centre, a focal point.'

While the band was winding its way around the country with Talking Heads, the search was on for a producer for the first album, not an easy task for an unknown band playing unfashionable music. The shortlist was just two names: Pete Gage, who used to play with Vinegar Joe, and Muff Winwood. Steve Winwood's brother had been a member of the Spencer Davis Group who had had a string of chart hits in the sixties, including the classic 'Gimme Some Loving', and was a respected producer. Winwood had the time, and the Straits went into Island Studios, in Basing Street, West London, on 14 February.

The material was basically the stage set, though one or two songs were omitted: 'Sacred Loving' from the original demo; 'Nadine', the

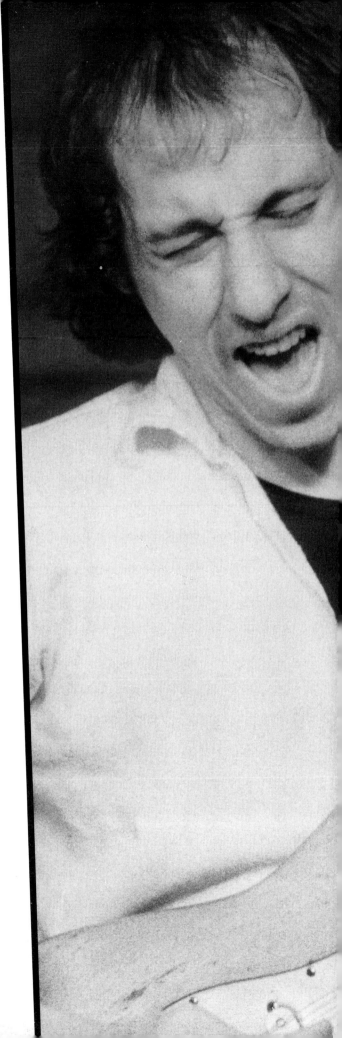

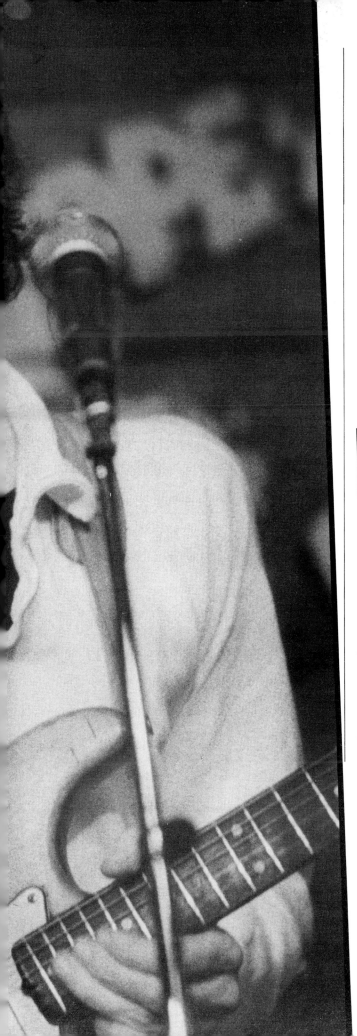

Chuck Berry encore; 'Real Girl', a jokey number with lyrics based on the personal ads in London listings magazine *Time Out;* and 'Eastbound Train', a straightforward boogie that was later to appear on a compilation album and as the B side of 'Sultans Of Swing'.

John continues: 'They gave us three weeks to do the whole album, which at the time seemed like a colossal amount of studio time, but of course it turned out that we needed an extra week, and after much wrangling they gave it to us. We knew all the songs backwards, virtually, but when we got into the studios we had to start at the bottom and work them all up. And when we'd skinned it all down, it just sounded a lot better, so that's why we kept it.'

Ed says: 'The two things I can remember were that Muff constantly asked Pick to play time rather than fills, and Pick kept getting pissed off with this. And the other thing was that Muff kept saying to them: "If you boys stick together, you'll do all right. Don't worry about it. Just stick together."

'In the haphazard way that these things happen, Muff had his studio time and his budget and I'm sure he went in with the attitude: "Let's just get this thing recorded." I mean, he accepted an extra £500 advance instead of an extra half per cent royalty, which subsequently was worth a great deal of money. He's very philosophical about that.

'There weren't many suggestions that outsiders could make about

Mark at the Hope & Anchor where 'Eastbound Train', the first song to appear on vinyl, was recorded

47

the album, really. The songs just stood for themselves. Nobody came along and said put synthesizers or a brass section on. John Stainze would try and chuck in a few suggestions, and Muff would make some, but basically what they recorded was what they'd been playing on tour. If you'd gone out and made a live recording there'd be virtually no difference.

'I don't influence the choice of songs. I might go to rehearsals and say: "I don't think this song's working," or whatever, but generally speaking, at that time, the musical end was very much up to them. Now it's up to Mark. Phonogram have never interfered artistically, but right from the start we've done things our way. It's very much like we're a little planet attached by an umbilical cord to Phonogram; we send the music up, and they send the records back down.'

Dire Straits, the eponymous debut album is a stunning achievement. Today, the music still sounds fresh and inspired. At the time it was a revelation, relaxing and stimulating, when all around were hustling for attention with express-train riffs repeated ad nauseam. It has the warm, uncomplicated feel of the best of American music of the time, eclectic in its influences. It draws from rock 'n' roll, country and blues, but remains lyrically and vocally very distinctively British. The playing, most noticeably from Mark, of course, is unfussy but inspired. For the first time in ages a guitarist had come along who had something *fresh* to say. If anything, the lead guitar is understated, heightening the dramatic moments with pauses rather than cluttering up every available space with chords.

Most noticeable of all, though, is that this is an album of strong, melodic songs. Everything else is harnessed to serve them. The album is arranged in chronological order, a sequence of events in Mark's life. The opening song, 'Down To The Waterline', harks back to Mark's memories of the River Tyne. The remaining four on the first side refer to unhappy love affairs; most probably they're all about the break-up of his marriage.

Thus, in the gentle 'Water Of Love' he sings: 'Once I had a woman I could call my own/Once I had a woman now my woman is gone'; in the sharp and spikey 'Setting Me Up': 'All you wanted was a piece of the action/Now you talk about another man'; in the brooding 'Six Blade Knife': 'Everybody got a knife it can be just what they want it to be/A needle, a wife or something that you just can't see'. In 'Southbound Again' he begins: 'That woman's with her lover boy/Never want to see her face again', but it ends on an optimistic note: 'Right now I'm sick of living/But I'm going to keep on trying'.

Side two takes the story into London, with 'Sultans of Swing', the most infectious and instantly memorable of the songs on the album. 'In The Gallery' follows, inspired by a visit to the art gallery with John but also built around a sculptor friend. And there are two songs rich in images taken from Mark's wanderings around the capital. 'Wild West End', a great crowd favourite from the early days of Dire Straits, and 'Lions', written at the time of recording.

But the songs have more in them than a personal view of Mark, his life and feelings: there's a universal message. 'Sultans', for example, is an acutely observed portrait of a specific amateur band, but it conveys the joys all musicians feel in creating and communicating. It was a debut that promised great things for the future.

With the album in the can, a small end-of-recording party was held for band and record company in a restaurant just down the Portobello Road from the studios. They had something to celebrate.

John, Mark, Pick and Dave: an early photo session after the completion of the first album

CHAPTER 4
Rockaway, Rockaway

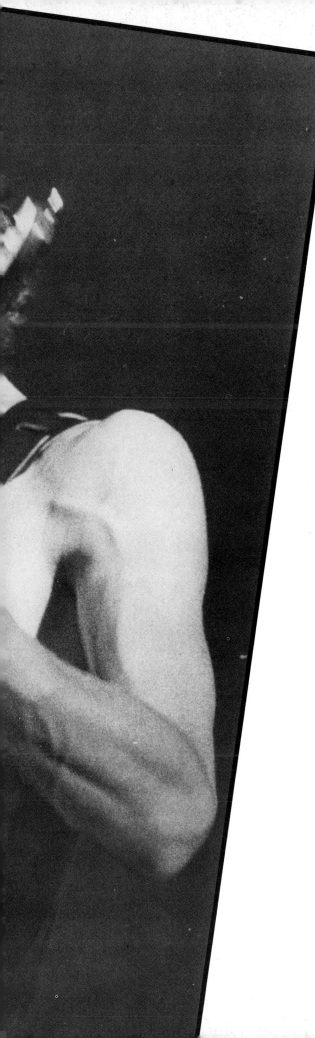

Dire Straits had a lot of things going for them – the songs, the musicianship and an attitude that made them look at their career in the long term rather than settling for a quick pay-off. But sometimes that's not enough; there are many greatly talented artists who have swum against the commercial tide and drowned. A little luck comes in handy, too.

The Straits' good fortune was that while they started off swimming in the wrong direction, the tide changed, and they found they weren't the only ones in the sea. Punk rock had thrown together some very unlikely bedfellows. For every ninety-second thunderbolt thrash in the old 'I hate everybody' story, a counterpoint emerged: Elvis Costello crafted songs of passion and intelligence; Graham Parker re-introduced the punch of R 'n' B; Madness and the 2-Tone label brought back sixties ska beat. Everybody was loosely grouped as new wave, and Dire Straits sheltered under that umbrella. They played London's Roundhouse, for example, early in 1978 alongside the frenetic punk idiocy of Slaughter and the Dogs, and the cool, intellectual rock of Talking Heads.

Their first song to appear on record was 'Eastbound Train', a live recording made at the Front Row Festival at London's Hope & Anchor pub in November 1977. On the ensuing live *Front Row Festival* compilation album, they were sandwiched between a whole variety of styles, from pure punk to rockabilly, reggae to rock. The only qualification for new wave was to be new, and to have a certain rough edge in live performance that avoided comparison with the hated pomp rock superstars.

Luckily, good songs weren't on the blacklist, and it's significant that of the seventeen different artists on the *Front Row* album, the only three who made any permanent mark – the Straits, XTC and the Stranglers – all relied on strong, individual material.

Ed underlines the point: 'There are a million guitar players who can stand on their heads in dry ice, spinning mirror balls with their feet while playing unbelievable licks. But you can only do that for a limited period of time. The things that live on are the songs, whether they're by Cole Porter, Barry Manilow, or whoever. Long after Dire Straits have stopped playing concerts, I hope that the songs will have made their mark.'

That was already happening. In March the Straits went into a residency at London's prestigious Marquee club. All the shows were sold out. The plan was for the album to be released in May, when a British tour supporting Climax Blues Band had been arranged. But in April the band were called into the office of Phonogram's managing director and asked to re-record 'Sultans of Swing' for a single. He felt that the album version was neither rough nor exciting enough.

Ed says: 'I never thought about them as a singles act; singles to me have always been the icing on the cake. It's only when you get into record companies and their marketing ideas that "That's the single!" crops up.

Phonogram were adamant that a single would help give the album a boost, so the band, still unconvinced, trooped up to Pathway studios and produced another version of 'Sultans' by themselves, with Chas as engineer. The single was set for May release, the album was postponed until 8 June.

Meanwhile, there were problems with the album, or rather its packaging. Ed says: 'There were endless arguments about the sleeve. The problem with Dire Straits is their attitude towards art, in inverted commas, which might be a photograph of them, videos, any way in which they're visually presented. There is no consensus about what constitutes good art. They don't know what it is until it's presented to them, so it's constantly a process of stabbing in the dark. At that point, the Phonogram art department had been assigned the sleeve and there were just unbelievable arguments.

'Finally, the group just gave in. The session which produced the back cover photos – and of all the pictures taken of them, these are probably the most widely circulated – took place in freezing cold conditions in a warehouse in South London at dawn one day. Nobody wanted to be there, never mind have his picture taken, so we have four particularly bad photos.'

Also born at this time, was the little red guitar, the child of artist Chuck Loyola, which became band logo, but has since been dropped.

'Sultans', coupled with 'Eastbound Train', was released in May and reached the Top Forty but soon dropped out while the band were on their somewhat unsuccessful British tour with Climax Blues Band. This was immediately followed by a European tour with American stadium rockers Styx, which turned out to be an unpleasant disaster.

John explains: 'They couldn't relate to the fact that they were huge in America and didn't mean dogshit anywhere else. We only played three gigs – Paris, the Hague, Hamburg – before they cut the tour short and went back home. Styx were unapproachable as people. They wouldn't even say hello to you in the lobby of the hotel. It was pathetic. I think they had a lot of group tension amongst themselves as well. I felt disappointed that we'd gone with such an abortionate bunch of people. It was a depressing tour; we were glad to get back.'

On their return, the album was released and received an enthusiastic thumbs up from most critics, but commercially it didn't set the world on fire immediately, peaking at number thirty-seven in the charts. The band set out on their first British headlining tour, playing mostly clubs and colleges.

Ed says: 'I went on the first part of the tour. It started at the dreadful Lafayette in Wolverhampton, and worked down from there. I can remember in one place somebody was sick in the bass bin and in deference to our roadie Pick and Mark cleaned it up. In another, the band drove round and round the gig trying to find it before realizing that the fish and chip shop was the gig and they had to get into the hall through the griddling area. But it was a very successful tour.'

Halfway through, Ed left for America to set up a record deal. Although the Phonogram contract was worldwide, it stipulated that the band could not be licensed to any American company controlled by Polygram (Phonogram's parent company) except RSO, basically because it was thought at the time that the American arm was in a shambles.

Although nobody could have foreseen it, this stipulation has had a direct effect on Dire Straits' fortunes in the United States, and, indirectly, on the band itself.

RSO, then the hottest label in the US with the Bee Gees' *Saturday Night Fever,* were duly offered the Straits, but failed to respond. Robert Allan took the album to Columbia (CBS) in New York, who were interested but wouldn't release it until Christmas.

Hotting up: John (top) and Dave as the band's first album starts to take off

Ed and Robert linked up in Los Angeles and started punting the album around. The priorities were to find a label with the right image – 'We didn't fit in with Journey and Santana at CBS; or Hall and Oates at RCA' – and also one that was willing to release the album fairly soon. The danger was that two major markets would be out of step with each other.

Two companies were really keen to sign: Mercury, Phonogram's American sister label, who were, in fact, contractually precluded from signing them, and Warner Brothers.

Ed says: 'Mercury pursued me around Los Angeles, and a person who was subsequently sacked offered me a huge bribe to get the band to change their minds about this clause. I have no idea whether the guy was authorized, but he offered me a six-figure amount. He took me into a sauna in a studio where City Boy were recording and offered me the bribe. I was so naive, I didn't know that he was serious until a few minutes after the conversation. He'd got incredibly bad breath and my overriding impression was: God, this guy stinks. I wish he'd take his six-figure sum and go away.

'Incidentally, later on I was offered half a million pounds in cash in any country in the world for Dire Straits' management contract, which I turned down. It isn't assignable anyway. And the person concerned totally missed the point of why I was doing it. It wasn't for the money.'

Ed and Robert had a more conventional reception at Warners, and thanks to the enthusiasm of Roberta Peterson and Karen Burgh, they were eventually signed.

Ed agrees. 'They really went out on a limb for us. And as it happens, Warners was the company we really wanted to be with, for no other reason than they'd got Randy Newman, Van Morrison, Bonnie Raitt and so on. Looking at labels, that's where we fitted.'

Ed flew back to England, to find that strange things were happening in Europe. The album and single trickled out during July in Holland and Belgium, and in Germany only the album was released. Then Ed started receiving telexes from Amsterdam: 'The album's done 3,000 . . . 6,000'. Then Brussels: 'It's done 1,500 . . . 1,700'. Nobody took much notice.

John: 'Then we had a call from Holland saying that "Sultans" was getting a fantastic amount of airplay and the album was selling. It eventually sold 50,000 copies there, a gold record. And Phonogram had said that if the first album sold 5,000 copies worldwide they'd be happy.

'We all thought, Jesus Christ, this is fantastic. So we got on a plane and went over there to do a presentation and a TV show called Pink Pop. There was a big black limousine at the airport and we thought, this is it. We've made it. We went shooting off to the TV studios, which was very exciting, cameramen everywhere, lights flashing. We played "Sultans" and went back to this big hotel in Amsterdam. We were really high on it, unbelievably high, really excited.

'Of course what we didn't realize was that we were letting ourselves in for a really tough time. They split us all up and wheeled in one journalist after another for ten to twelve hours. There was no food, and every mini-bar in every single room was emptied; we just got more and more pissed and tired. It seemed like we were being pummelled by these journalists and we let it happen.

'Round about one in the morning it was suggested that the band should eat. We went downstairs to this club in the hotel, and Ed flipped, lost his marbles. Everybody was really ratty and drunk. It was terrible, but at the same time it was very exciting. The next day there were photo sessions and all this business.

'The trip taught us that we weren't going to get inundated with millions of interviews again. But you learn all the time. It never happened again – until we got to Italy, of course, and you just can't control the Italians.

'We've always had the philosophy that we'll talk to anybody, doesn't matter who it is, given the amount of time we've got and given that we've got something to say. There are occasions when we don't have much we want to talk about. I realize that everybody wants to talk to the main-man, Mark, but that's never worried me. It's quite natural – everybody wants to talk to Mick Jagger and Keith Richards in the Stones.'

Even though the first album was just beginning to pick up steam, thoughts now turned to the next. The question arose again: who would produce? And then Jerry Wexler, a legendary figure since the fifties for his work recording R 'n' B artists and his connections with Atlantic Records, offered his services after picking up the buzz for the band from Warners.

Ed says: 'I remember saying to Mark: "How about Jerry Wexler?" And Mark said: "Who's Jerry Wexler?" So I said: "Ben E. King, the Drifters, Aretha Franklin, Solomon Burke, Ray Charles . . ." And he said: "Fine. Sounds like a good idea".'

Ed and Mark flew out to cement the deal and finalize plans in Muscle Shoals, Alabama, the home of a recording studio much favoured by soul and R 'n' B artists and anyone who wants to sound like them, and an accompanying cast of eminent session musicians.

Ed goes on: 'Jerry picked us up outside our hotel in a pick-up truck. He made us feel very welcome and drove us off to see the Tennessee Valley Authority dam project, and spouted on about the land and history. We were like two kiddies at the knee of Ernest Hemingway, who Jerry closely resembles.

'We went off to a truckstop and sitting in there were all these Muscle Shoals musicians. We had our griddle, our salted ham, which made us sick, and our grits, which made us sick again, and then went off to the studio. By this time it was midday and the cast for a Mavis Staples record was assembling.

'It turned out that they'd already done most of the tracks and Mavis was flying in that day from a gig in Chicago with Pops (her father, and leader of the Staples Singers). She was going to do the vocals in three days and go back on the road. Mark and I were amazed that this was the way they were doing it. When Mavis arrived, Jerry told her how to sing the songs, which again we thought was amazing. They were changing the lyrics of a Doobie Brothers song and cutting stuff about. Barry Beckett was there, directing the musicians, and we were watching from the control box.

'Finally, Barry said to Mark: "Would you like to play?" So Mark nervously took hold of Jimmy Johnson's guitar and went and played on "Lies", the J.J. Cale song, which he knew.'

Mark says: 'It sounded real good, too. I remember Pop Staples. I was sitting in the studio, playing, and Pop came in and he looked down at me. I thought, What am I doing? I turned to Barry, who said to me: "The guy thinks you're amazing. He just freaked. The guy's frightened. You've just made him miserable." And Pop said to me: "You're too damn good, son." I was a little bit overawed by it all. I

Right: Practice makes perfect. Mark working on *Communiqué* at Compass Point, Nassau

Below: *Communiqué* producers Barry Beckett (left) and Jerry Wexler

mean, I didn't really know what a chart was, or anything like that. I was just strumming along.'

It was agreed with Jerry and Barry that the second Dire Straits album would be recorded at Compass Point studios, at Nassau in the Bahamas. The producers didn't want to travel too far from the States, while the band now preferred to record outside the UK for tax reasons.

Business over, Mark and Ed moved on to California, to meet the people at Warners in Burbank, who were then in the throes of discomania and more anxious to get on with Bootsy Collins records than to spend time on a new English band. Ed reckons: 'It was the "shit against the fan" attitude. The album was just going to spew out of the machine. Mark and I did our bit, which was basically a PR exercise. But this is what you do with a record company: you love them to death and then they'll get motivated.'

But the action, saleswise, was happening in Europe, and in October the Straits went off to tour Belgium, Holland and Germany. It was obvious that the band were very big news indeed. Originally planned as a club tour, it was hastily moved into halls because of the huge ticket demand. A Belgian promoter went one step further, and moved the show from a club, to a hall, to a tent in a field, and the Straits played before 2,500, in a town where they were expecting 300. The whole tour was completely sold out, and by the time they reached Hamburg and Berlin, they were playing 2,000-seat halls.

A British university tour followed, with a couple of city halls thrown in, and the band debuted the new material that was to appear on *Communiqué*. It sold out, despite the fact that *Dire Straits* and 'Sultans' had disappeared five months previously. Meanwhile the rest of the world was getting the message. The album came out in the US on 20 October, and on 9 November Jerry Wexler sent this encouraging message: 'Initial airplay reaction widespread and impressive.' Australia and New Zealand picked up on the album, which made number one in both countries by Christmas.

At the end of November, the band flew out to Nassau, and stepped straight into a different world. Their surroundings were ultra-luxurious; they stayed in Capricorn, a mansion belonging to a millionaire arts patron, with swimming pool, Greek porticos, statues of black manikins and Wedgwood china. In the evenings they would sit in a marbled dining-room beneath a crystal chandelier, eating huge meals personally supervised by Jerry, waited on hand and foot.

Ed says: 'Wexler sat at the end of the table just like Ernest Hemingway, regaling us with anecdotes. We all sat around, little blue-eyed boys; it was very weird. Then we would go and have coffee and brandy in the lounge, play back the day's tapes and then listen to Django Reinhardt records, or Blind Pegleg Loser, or something. Or we'd spend an evening sipping lime juice with Robert Palmer and his wife, who lived there. We were borrowing Robert's amps because all the studio ones were useless.'

The work schedule was fairly well regimented. Starting early in the afternoon, they worked through most evenings. All the songs bar 'Communiqué', which was written at Compass Point one afternoon while engineer Jack Nuber was sick, had been demo'd in London. So impressive were these that Jerry would joke: 'You made the album in the first place. Now we just have to remake it.'

Any initial qualms that Mark may have had about working with

Where do you think you're going? Mark in Nassau

Jerry were soon lost: 'I thought there might be a possibility – this was before we'd sent Jerry the demos – that we might be pressurized into excessive use of other instruments, though I felt all right about it at root. I thought, never mind, because I know it can't be a bad record – not really. In fact, what happened was that he was the first to say that there should be nothing added. All the talk about using the Memphis Horns was unnecessary.'

The way the production team worked was quickly obvious. Barry Beckett, a brilliant keyboards player and producer whose career at Muscle Shoals stretched back to James and Bobby Purify's soul classic 'I'm Your Puppet', took charge of the musical end, while Jerry was more of an organizer.

Mark explains: 'It's a whole feel thing, understanding pick-ups, times, choice of take, a sheer response to the cadence of something, sometimes a knowledge that something's not a goer. Jerry is also there for a vibe and a sure-fire feeling that when he's not there, he has left a space. And the other important thing is that Jerry handles the vocals.'

Wexler, with an amazing string of hits behind him, was obviously a producer of the old school, as Ed noted. 'I was talking to the band at the dining-table one day about money, and he said, in front of them: "You should never discuss business with the artist". That's the difference between his era and my era – the band and I have no secrets. I don't handle their money; I don't want to handle their money. All the time they know totally what's going on.

'Jerry's attitude was, it was like when he was recording with Mavis Staples. The artist was a tool for him, in the same way that the guitar player or the tape operator was. Mavis Staples had no say at all in the choice of songs, or the way she sang them – yet it came out as a Mavis Staples album. With her, and the Straits, Jerry was like the patriarchal figure sitting in the control box. I remember he actually fell asleep one day.'

Right: The old rocking-chair: Mark tunes up in Nassau

For his part, Jerry was much taken with Dire Straits. 'They have that Southern characteristic. It's a porous, breathing track where you don't fill it up. Making music is always a trade-off between how much you state and how much you leave to the imagination, and the answer to that is your own taste.

'It's impossible for me to categorize the band. There just isn't any analogue. Almost always you can put somebody into a box and say: "They're like so-and-so." This band is not like anybody I can think of. So the next step in the syllogism is: don't mess with it, don't spoil it – and I don't think that would even be an option, because Mark wouldn't permit it.

'Mark doesn't play that kind of screaming, mindless guitar that's been so popular, which depends on just the sheer flights of the sound. But he improvises melodically, which to me is the hallmark of a great musician, as opposed to just improvising within the chord structure and being harmonically oriented. He can do that and still have a famliar relationship to the song. The ghost of the song is always there. That's good improvisation, in my opinion.

'Dire Straits represent a very contemporary aspect of British society. They're young and for the most part quite well-educated people, with a very strong sense of self and where their best interests lie. There are elements of a certain consciousness, of maybe a lower-middle-class and working-class outlook with the benefit of college education, and it's very good because it's a view that's anti-Establishment without a lot of blatant sloganeering.'

The album itself – the title *Communiqué* was chosen despite strong pressure from Jerry for *News* – very much reflects the circumstances under which it was made. It's not a city album, but soft and langourous, gently fashioned under a hot sun. It also has echoes from the debut album.

Ed has a theory. 'I think Jerry, and to a certain extent, Barry, was trying to copy the sound of the first record, but he wanted to sweeten it up a bit for American radio. So he would come into the studio and ask Mark what amp he used on "In The Gallery", or what guitar; could they get the same kind of setting? what drumheads did Pick use? And they would go in the next day and imitate the sounds of the first LP, but it was almost like they put them through a machine and made them smoother.'

Communiqué is Dire Straits' most controversial album. It polarized the critics and is still regarded by many as either too much like the first LP or too laid back. Of course there are similarities with *Dire Straits:* it's the same band, with keyboards added by Barry Beckett (credited on the sleeve as B. Bear), and the same writer. But in structure, and in the style of writing this is a very different album.

Not all the songs here are about Mark Knopfler – on the first album, all but 'Sultans of Swing' mention either 'I' or 'me' – and the themes are more abstract. This is especially true of 'Once Upon A Time In The West', which opens the LP with a similar teasing guitar line as the one on 'Down To The Waterline' but then breaks into a chugging beat that seems to run through the whole of the first side, linking it together.

'News' is often interpreted as harking back to Mark's days as a reporter; in fact it was inspired by a news item about a motorcyclist dying in a road crash. 'Communiqué' is the journalist's song, littered with newspaper expressions and clichés: 'no comment', 'incommunicado', 'rumours are flying', 'speculation (is) rife', 'serious

The band with *Communiqué* co-producer Barry Beckett – he worked mainly on the music; Jerry Wexler was the organizer

piece'. But it's also about Mark's reactions to being interviewed, a hot news item, albeit seen through a distancing 'he' rather than as 'I': 'Maybe he could talk about the tricks of the trade/Maybe he could talk about himself/Maybe he could talk about the money he made/Maybe he could say something else'.

With the first LP, the stories in the songs were more cut and dried, vignettes of experience; now they're less clear. In 'Where Do You Think You're Going', the affair is left up in the air: does she leave, or does she stay?

The second side bears more relationship to *Dire Straits*: five distinct songs, separately parcelled. The 'Lady Writer' is authoress Marina Warner, whose appearance on a TV show brings back unhappy memories of a love now gone (possibly Mark's wife), and there's real venom in it: 'Remember that you never read a book', and 'You talked to me when you felt like it'. The tune is very similar to 'Sultans', which may explain why it flopped when issued as a single.

'Portobello Belle' harks back to 'Wild West End' and 'Lions'; this time the journey is around the Portobello Road. 'Single-Handed Sailor' was written around the band's rehearsal studio in Greenwich – 'On a night when the wind is wailing around the *Cutty Sark*' – and the atmospheric 'Follow Me Home' refers back to an incident in Mark's past.

'Angel Of Mercy' is a genuine rarity: a happy love song. No problems, no angst, no bust-ups, just a fun relationship.

Interviewed at Compass Point by Ian Birch of *Melody Maker*, Mark talked about the changes in his writing technique. 'I feel more of a detachment now from 'me' in a song, which doesn't detract from the song. It's just a rock song. I don't feel that I should have to answer for it – I'm not trying to negate my own responsibility for the songs completely, but there's a whole load of natural good licks that take on a life of their own, in terms of their cohesiveness, yet still leave all kinds of open ends for chance or whatever might crop up.

'I think that applies to a lot of people who write and play. There's a sense in which songs are like other people. You can't own them, or say that *this* is what was intended, because you'd be a liar. It's contradictory, I know, because the whole thing is coming from you anyway. But when somebody does a portrait, for instance, I'd be very surprised if the level at which it comes out resembled what they photographically intended, if you like.

'It's a nice discovery to make, actually. I don't know if you've ever found that a thing might begin to take shape of its own accord, either by the dictates of the formulae that you've decided to use or just through the sheer multiplicity of the content, or I don't know what. What I'm saying is that you've never got anything mapped out completely. Given that, I think what you *do* need is a feeling for format, but what I really want to avoid is all the personal attention on Mark the bloke, who is *just a bloke*. I really don't want any of that shit.

'Sometimes when I listen to these songs I think they've got nothing to do with me as a bloke. For instance, "Follow Me Home" is very important in a lot of ways. Yes, I was on an island, and yes, there was a girl – but it's not very different from any other tourist sleeping on a beach, going up to a ruin looking out over the sea, eating meat and drinking wine. But the idea goes beyond that, leading to a song which doesn't actually belong to the bloke. I like to be divorced, in that sense, from the song.'

Events, however, were to change that.

CHAPTER 5

Getting Crazy on the Waltzers

'Here I am, less than a year after signing a deal, sitting in Nassau: ginger ale, fag, half a million albums under my belt, second album being produced by two of the best producers going – where's the pressure? Do you see any pressure?'

Dave Knopfler, December 1978

The picture most outsiders have of successful rock stars is that of a bunch of greedy parasites who lounge around in luxury and idleness, emerging every now and again to whinge and whine about how tough life is at the top. Their 'work' consists of writing songs, recording them in studios crammed full of instruments that can create every conceivable sound, and standing on a stage for two hours a night.

When musicians talk about pressure – and they frequently do – most people assume they mean that the record company keeps nagging them to write the songs faster.

That view takes no account of the creative process, which doesn't work in the same way as a production line. The lyrics to 'In The Gallery' may have been written in the back of a car in a couple of hours, but other songs have taken weeks or months to put together.

And as soon as success comes, particularly on the huge, worldwide scale of Dire Straits' first album and single, then the pressure is self-applied. The pressure is on the writer, in the first instance, to come up with songs that are as good, if not better, than their predecessors – not only for his own sake, but for those millions who will be disappointed if he doesn't. Which immediately begs the question: what made the songs *that* good in the first place?

There's no way of telling. And so self-doubt creeps in. Is this song as good as that song, when I don't really know *why* it was so good in the first place? A line appears: should I write exactly what I think, or should I write what I think people want to hear? Am I an isolated individual writing for myself, or am I a communicator, translating my thoughts into a form that others can understand?

This is the pressure on the individual, but Dire Straits are also a performing band, in which there has to be a group cohesiveness to make it all work. Touring means working and living together. Inevitably tensions become exacerbated, and as each member of the band tries to keep his own end up, he exerts pressure on the others.

Mark was like a playwright who also directed and acted in his play. The group, as they prepared to go out on the road again in February 1979, became a travelling circus. The actual playing was no different, but success brought with it an endless series of promotional extras: interviews, photo sessions, visits to radio stations and record companies, glad-handing after gigs, receptions, hanging around TV studios, and adulation. Everyone wanted to know them – they were stars!

It's very difficult to keep a level head when everyone wants to take a piece of it home as a souvenir. Inevitably, some members of the band handled the fame better than others as the crazy fairground ride careered up and down from October 1978 until it came to a shuddering halt in December 1979.

Ed takes up the story: 'Musically, as they became bigger, little insecurities started to show themselves. And it got to the point where some people in the band were ashamed of other people in the band. They didn't want outsiders to perceive how the finished product actually got there, like actors who don't like people going to rehearsals.

'Pick, for example, some of the time had a slightly snobbish

Musical empathy on-stage, but off-stage the tension was growing between Mark and Dave

attitude to the ability of John and David. He thought Mark was a great
guitarist and he loved playing Mark's songs, but he felt that we
would have been better off with a second guitar player. This would
show itself in the odd rows, the odd ultimatums, the odd "if he doesn't
go, I'm going" sort of thing.'

John says: 'Of course, there's always conflict in bands. I'd say this
band gets along exceptionally well, and always has done. But I think
it would be impossible not to have moments of tension as well,
because you're living with the same people all the time. It's almost
like a marriage: you have to give and take a hell of a lot, and if you're
not big enough to do that then you don't stay in a band.'

Dave feels the pattern is familiar. 'All the things that I remember

The circus comes to town: high pressure
touring in 1979

66

as a kid, all the things you read about in the music papers, about what happens to people – you somehow think you're immune to that. You assume that because you start from a different place, you won't find yourself going in that direction. And it doesn't seem to be the case. You start out with one idea and lose sight of it as the pressures lead you along that path towards the same old bullshit that every other band's been through.'

The actual construction of the band, meanwhile, was undergoing a subtle change away from its democratic roots. Ed noticed that Mark was growing in confidence, becoming almost dictatorial – 'and I mean that in the nicest possible sense, not in the fascist sense, because I think that his dictatorialism is a huge benefit.'

1979 started with the mixing of *Communiqué* in Muscle Shoals, followed by TV performances, promotion, interviews and rehearsals for a short tour of Germany and Holland, which acted as a warm-up for the first American tour.

Touring by now was no simple matter, and Paul Cummins, somewhat reluctantly at first, joined up to sort out the complex details. An experienced tour manager, he had worked with Gallagher & Lyle, Linda Lewis, Andy Fairweather-Low, Jesse Winchester and XTC.

'I was caught up in new wave at the time, Talking Heads more than anyone else. I wasn't really into the Straits' first album, but I was with the B-52s down in Georgia and it was being played everywhere. I remember thinking, this band is going to be huge.'

He first saw the Straits at the end of their British tour in Hitchin in November 1978. 'New wave was still happening and there were two punks down the front, spitting at Mark while he was doing "Water Of Love", and bashing the microphone into his mouth. The band stopped the number, which I thought was really unprofessional. If you dared stop a punk gig in those days, you died.

'Then Pete Murdoch got up on stage and said: "The band refuse to play any more until the troublemakers leave the hall." I was cowering on the side of the stage, waiting for a riot, but the crowd opened up like it was the Red Sea, the punks left and got the shit beaten out of them out the front. I thought he handled it very well, because I wouldn't dream of stopping a gig. The old saga of the show must go on. I'd get a couple of security guys to stick a gun in their back or something and force them out.

'I got to know the band very well in America. They'd never had a tour manager before, and he can make an incredible difference. It was mainly because I'd toured before, I knew the ropes. I don't like getting ripped off, or hotels that take money off you and don't give any service. I believe in getting service.

'There's a great deal of moral feeling towards an act when you're its tour manager – I mean, you'd kill for your artist. You'd kill to get the show on time. I'd throw dreadful wobblers and I'd scream at these people who were six-feet-four and weighed twenty stone. They'd look at me and couldn't believe that I was doing this.'

John says: 'America was our first real taste of the crazy side of the music business. It was ridiculous, unbelievably exciting. It was a club tour and it was a real hot, happening thing.'

Ed agrees: 'It was an amazing experience. It wasn't exactly the second coming of the Beatles, but it was a big deal. Because we had decided to stay in the clubs, there was an even bigger buzz, it had scarcity value.'

Above. Mark takes the strain – manager Ed Bicknell relaxes for a moment

It was also completely exhausting – fifty-one shows in thirty-eight days, over 300 interviews and countless visits to radio stations to promote the album and single. It paid off, too. *Dire Straits* reached number two in the Billboard albums chart. 'Sultans' became a Top Five single. Ed continues: 'Warners, and I don't blame them, got hold of a mallet and they whacked the lemon as hard and as often as they could. You see, Dire Straits were the first British band to break in America on that scale since the days of groups like Zeppelin and Tull.'

In New York, the band sold out the prestigious Bottom Line club so fast they were asked to play the gigantic Madison Square Gardens. They stayed in the club, which was packed wall-to-wall with celebrities.

For Mark, it was an extraordinary experience. 'All the stars have these minders, great big blokes who make sure their artists aren't touched or pestered by ordinary mortals. Suddenly this gigantic bouncer starts pushing his way through – people are being knocked out of the way, into each other's drinks and this guy's shouting: "Make way for Carly Simon! Make way for Carly Simon!"'

Among the backstage visitors was Gary Katz, a noted producer then working with Steely Dan on their new album, *Gaucho,* at New York's Sigma Sound Studios. Would Mark be interested in playing a session? he asked. He would indeed, for Mark had been an admirer of the band from the start and had seen them when they'd played in London.

What he found in the studio, though, was a completely alien system of working: endless takes, with Donald Fagen and Walter Becker trying to tell him how to play. 'I'd be there and Walter and Donald would be saying: "Can *he* do this, or can *he* do that?" referring to me while I was standing there. I know now that that's how Americans talk sometimes. They were talking like I'd been brought in to provide this kind of service. In a way it wasn't too different from a drain-cleaning operation.'

The results can be heard on the song 'Time Out Of Mind', which quite graphically illustrates the split between the Americans and the British guitarist. Mark is kept low in the mix, in one channel, and plays a line that worries itself around the melody, complementing the tune rather than repeating it. Like a veteran stage actor, he performs a neat piece of theatrical business that attracts the attention without interrupting the play.

Ed drily comments on the session: 'When you're a rather naive English person, you've come in on your first American tour and the world's falling around your ears, and here you are, sitting with Steely Dan and they're talking about you as if you're not in the room, it's very strange.'

During the tour, 'Sultans Of Swing' finally broke into the charts in Britain, and there were frantic appeals for the band to come back and promote it and the album. They were ignored, and the tour carried on to Los Angeles and another prestigious club date at the Roxy. Here the audience was even more star-studded: Rod Stewart, Dave Mason, Linda Ronstadt, Keith Richards, Ronnie Wood, Bette Midler, Jackson Browne and Russ Kunkel were there. And so was Bob Dylan.

Dylan was in the process of setting up the recording of a new album, to be produced by the *Communiqué* team of Jerry Wexler and Barry Beckett. In an exclusive upstairs bar at the Roxy, Mark and Pick were asked if they'd like to play on the sessions. Of course they would.

What wasn't apparent at the time was what kind of album it was going to be; Bob Dylan's conversion to Christianity had been reported – this was at a time when, in the wake of President Jimmy Carter, many Americans were becoming born-again Christians – but nobody knew whether it would have any effect on his music.

Ed says: 'I got saddled with Dylan's mate, who said to me: "I've just been on a tour in Europe. I had a really great time." So I said: "Oh, what band are you with?" He said: "I'm not with a band, I'm with the Children of God." And I went: "Aaaaah." I didn't think any more about it then.'

The tour carried on for a few more days, ending at the University of Davis, Sacramento, on 2 April. Paul remembers: 'When we finished that tour I wanted to die. Everyone got very close. As individuals, they rubbed me up the wrong way from the point of business because they knew so much more about the rock 'n' roll business than I did. I couldn't understand why these people were telling me that I was doing it all wrong. It wasn't so much me, as other things that the record company was doing.

'It wasn't until the end of that tour that success really started to home in on them, after everyone from the rock 'n' roll archives came out to the Roxy to see the band. Then it really dawned on them that they were destined for it. As individuals, Mark always knew what he wanted, and Pick and John were lovely guys, but David – I couldn't believe that he was older than me. He was unbearable from the word go. Whatever we did was always a problem.'

While the rest of the Straits took a break, Mark went back to Los Angeles and down to Dylan's Santa Monica studio to help work out the material. Dylan would plonk out rudimentary chords on the piano while Mark plugged in a guitar, and then they'd go into the songs.

They linked up with Pick, Jerry, Barry and bassist Tim Drummond

Mark, ever-growing in confidence

in Muscle Shoals at the beginning of May for the recording proper. Early in the sessions, Mark phoned Ed to say: 'It's going really well. The first night was pretty awful, it just didn't happen, but once we got into it, it was good. But all these songs are about God . . .'

Slow Train Coming is in no way a collection of hymns. It's a sinuous weaving of musical moods and styles that promotes individual discovery of God rather than the tub-thumping crusade of a righteous fundamentalist preacher. Some of the songs have no overt message, but when taken in context the subject matter is not hard to fathom.

The music is basic but rich in melody, rock crossed with R 'n' B and scattered with wailing Gospel harmonies from three soulful backing singers: Carolyn Dennis, Helena Springs and Regina Havis. Energy is punched in by the Muscle Shoals Horns while a tonking piano brings back echoes of old-time religion. The overall sound is stripped to the roots, sleek and glistening with craftsmanship, totally unlike the impassioned, haphazard instrumentation Dylan had used before. He described *Slow Train Coming* as his first professional album.

The environment was tailor-made for Mark, his guitar dancing softly around the theme of 'Gotta Serve Somebody" and luxuriating in the melody of 'Precious Angel'. His playing on the title track is a masterpiece of understatement, leaving wide open spaces which serve to emphasize the richness of what he does play. Pick keeps it

Constant touring and a broken romance: the strain starts to show

all together with an iron beat, embellishing the songs with delicate flourishes.

Mark and Pick managed to steer clear of the mauling Dylan received from the Press when the album appeared in 1979. Once again he had shrugged off the mantle of predictability and confounded the critics.

Meanwhile, the Straits were facing a major career decision. *Communiqué* was recorded, mixed and ready to go in June, a year to the day after *Dire Straits*. But in America the first album had only been out for seven months, and Warners thought there was still life in it; in particular, they wanted to release 'Down To The Waterline' as a follow-up to 'Sultans'. There was no question this time of a staggered release. The band were so hot, America would be flooded with imports.

It boiled down to either an artistic decision – release *Communiqué* – or a commercial decision – delay it. The release went ahead and, as often happens to follow-ups, it got panned by the critics and in America collided on its way up with *Dire Straits* coming down, creating confusion in the minds of many record-buyers. As a result, *Communiqué* sold only 350,000 copies in the States, compared with 1.2 million for the first album. Worldwide, it still sold by the million but never reached the level of its predecessor.

But while there were problems in America, Europe just couldn't get enough of Dire Straits. The band did a triumphant homecoming tour of Britain – where the single, 'Lady Writer', also failed to emulate 'Sultans', making it only to number fifty-one in the Music Week chart – sandwiched between appearances on the European festival circuit. In Holland they played before 60,000 (sharing the bill with Police and Elvis Costello), did four sell-out shows with Barclay James Harvest in Germany and two festivals in Belgium with Rory Gallagher.

Summer over, a second visit to the US had been arranged to start on 8 September. It could hardly have been fixed for a worse time, though Ed, who had booked the dates some months previously, could not have foreseen that *Communiqué* would not get the success it deserved, nor that the American music business would begin to slump dramatically.

'It was the first big hiccup since the days of *Saturday Night Fever*. In particular, the bottom dropped with a thud out of the concert market. Just as we arrived, large numbers of unemployed kids stopped going to concerts.'

The effect was not immediately apparent, as the East Coast strongholds of Boston, New York, Philadelphia and Washington all sold out. But the strain of constant touring was having an effect on the members of the band, particularly Mark.

Paul reveals: 'I was really worried about him. He wasn't eating. He was terribly pale. He was tired all the time. He was hot all the time. He was losing weight. I thought maybe he was losing salt because he was sweating so much. In Philadelphia I insisted he see a doctor. After the examination, the doctor came out and said: "I gave him a vitamin shot and he's fine. His problem is, he misses his girlfriend."'

The girlfriend was Holly Vincent, leader of a band called Holly and the Italians, who were managed by Ed and Paul. Holly was currently rehearsing in England.

Paul continues: 'I called her up and said: "Look, Holly, I know this isn't fair. It's up to you, but Mark's really depressed about being out here without you. It would be good if we could surprise him and get you on a flight out." And she said: "To tell you the truth, I was about to finish it all with Mark. I'm just about to tell him it's all over." I didn't really want to find that out. Mark was in a daze about her, completely love-struck.

'He called her literally minutes before he went on-stage that night, and she must have told him. I didn't know anything about it. But when he started to play "Where Do You Think You're Going" to finish the show I could see that something was wrong. He sang that song like he'd never sung it before or since. I was nearly crying.'

Mark went into a deep depression, every day sitting on his own on the tour bus, up front by the driver, barely communicating with anyone. The mood spread, exacerbated as they went south by half-empty halls. From Greensboro and Charlotte in North Carolina, through to Tampa and Miami in Florida, the tour tailed off to a sorry end.

The last three months of 1979 were a nightmare. Mark couldn't go back to Deptford and so stayed at Ed's flat in the Barbican, which inspired a song, 'Suicide Towers': Sitting up here/In Suicide Towers/Days and days/Hours and hours/I'm getting outta here/I'm going outta the door/Ain't going outta no window.' The riff later appeared as 'Expresso Love'.

New songs had been appearing and reappearing all the time on the US tour. 'Twisting By The Pool' was used as an encore, 'What's The Matter With You Baby' co-written with Dave some time back, got as far as a demo, but 'Suicide Towers', 'Sucker For Punishment', 'In My Car' and 'Bernadette', on which Dave sang lead vocal, have never surfaced.

Of the songs that were to make up the third album, only 'Solid Rock' and 'Les Boys' were performed on-stage in 1979. A number called 'Making Movies' was written and later transformed into 'Skateaway' but gave the LP its title. In addition, in the period at the end of '79/early '80, Mark produced demos of 'Solid Rock' and 'Twisting By The Pool' at Basing Street for a possible single that never appeared. He also produced an unreleased single for Lee Fardon.

In November, the band toured Europe, making their debut appearances in Scandinavia. The tour was hugely successful but, says Ed: 'The show was getting stale. Everybody had been working too hard, had got interview-itis, TV-itis. That period was just awful, it was fucking dreadful. I would say they were very close to breaking up. In fact, the momentum of what they were doing probably stopped it because nobody really had time to think.'

A few days off, and then four concerts in Ireland; a short break, and then two concerts at Lewisham Odeon and two at London's Rainbow would take them up to Christmas.

Ed remembers: 'Just before the London shows, Mark rang up and said: "I can't do these." There was much worrying and persuasion and eventually it got sorted out and the concerts went ahead. I knew at that point that we had got to stop. We were all going nuts. It was all sorts of trivia, but everything became a big problem. Getting the washing done was a big problem. Girlfriends were a huge problem.'

Mark now looks back on that period as 'an all-time low. I thought the band might split up, but I knew I'd be fine. I knew I was going on and that was it. Basically, if you look at everything that we've been

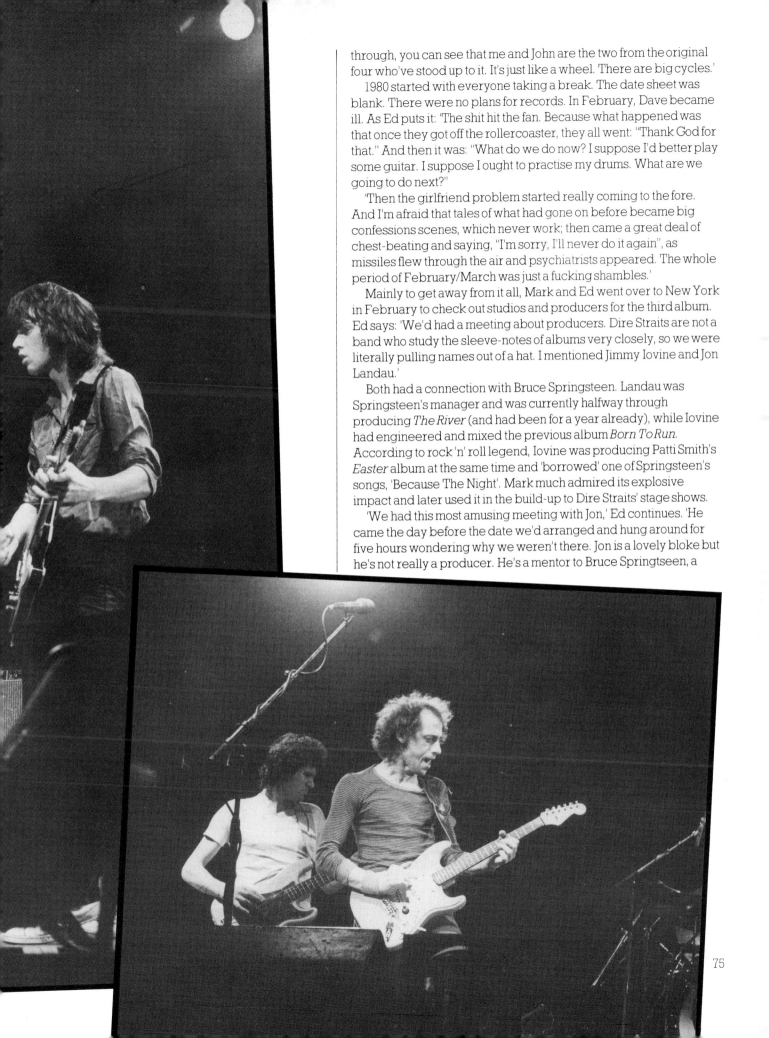

through, you can see that me and John are the two from the original four who've stood up to it. It's just like a wheel. There are big cycles.'

1980 started with everyone taking a break. The date sheet was blank. There were no plans for records. In February, Dave became ill. As Ed puts it: 'The shit hit the fan. Because what happened was that once they got off the rollercoaster, they all went: "Thank God for that." And then it was: "What do we do now? I suppose I'd better play some guitar. I suppose I ought to practise my drums. What are we going to do next?"

'Then the girlfriend problem started really coming to the fore. And I'm afraid that tales of what had gone on before became big confessions scenes, which never work; then came a great deal of chest-beating and saying, "I'm sorry, I'll never do it again", as missiles flew through the air and psychiatrists appeared. The whole period of February/March was just a fucking shambles.'

Mainly to get away from it all, Mark and Ed went over to New York in February to check out studios and producers for the third album. Ed says: 'We'd had a meeting about producers. Dire Straits are not a band who study the sleeve-notes of albums very closely, so we were literally pulling names out of a hat. I mentioned Jimmy Iovine and Jon Landau.'

Both had a connection with Bruce Springsteen. Landau was Springsteen's manager and was currently halfway through producing *The River* (and had been for a year already), while Iovine had engineered and mixed the previous album *Born To Run*. According to rock 'n' roll legend, Iovine was producing Patti Smith's *Easter* album at the same time and 'borrowed' one of Springsteen's songs, 'Because The Night'. Mark much admired its explosive impact and later used it in the build-up to Dire Straits' stage shows.

'We had this most amusing meeting with Jon,' Ed continues. 'He came the day before the date we'd arranged and hung around for five hours wondering why we weren't there. Jon is a lovely bloke but he's not really a producer. He's a mentor to Bruce Springtseen, a

friend and confidant. Mark was really looking for a technical
producer who could get sounds; in other words, an engineer.'

It was agreed that the problem with previous Straits albums was
that they had never achieved the electrifying effect of the stage
shows where the audience would expect to hear a laid-back J.J.
Cale sound, but would instead get a full-blown rock 'n' roll band.
Mark wanted the third album to bridge that gap. Iovine, with a track
record that included producing Tom Petty and Graham Parker,
seemed the man to do it.

Ed recalls Jimmy's appearance at the Mayflower hotel in New
York. 'He was dressed like Action Man, in a yellow suit and
appeared to be on speed, though I later realized that he takes bee
pollen, which has the same effect. He and Mark hit it off pretty well
from the start. Jimmy had some good ideas about how to achieve
sounds, and there were very intricate discussions about how to
amplify an acoustic guitar.'

It was agreed that Jimmy would produce the next album, although
when that would be, or what was to be on it, was left open. By now,
their record contract had been re-negotiated, so the band paid for
recording costs. Ed had to negotiate a fee for Iovine's services.

'Jimmy's manager wanted an extraordinary sum, a sum so great
that I spontaneously lost my temper and told him to fuck off. And he
said: "Well, that's what my client's been offered to produce
Foreigner." My comment was: "He doesn't want to produce
Foreigner."

'There was a lot of to-ing and fro-ing, and finally it was agreed that
Jimmy would do it for a figure that was quite viable given that he was
a hot producer, and in America, of course, producers are a hook for
the record company to hang their clothes on. We were coming off a
very weak record as far as the States were concerned.'

In early March the band assembled for the filming of a TV

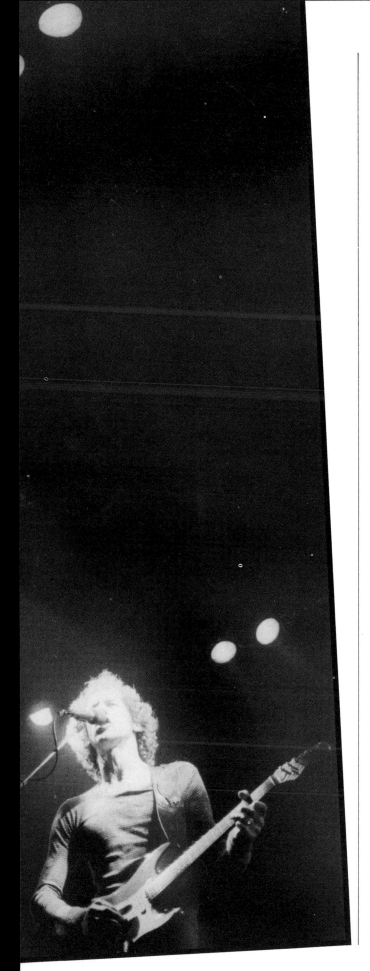

documentary about Dire Straits for BBC2's *Arena*. It incorporated footage of the Rainbow concerts and showed them rehearsing and demoing new material like 'Solid Rock' and 'Making Movies'. It also featured a fantasy video of 'Twisting By The Pool', and contained some revealing comments on their careers to date.

John talked about the tensions that emerged. '[Success] puts incredible pressure on you. Pick described it to me as an obstacle course, which I suppose really sums it up. You're a bit crazy for a while. One minute you're in America, the next minute you're in Germany, then you're making an album, then you're making some more music somewhere else and you never have time to stop and think. So for two years we've been in somewhat of a turmoil, working wherever we can, as hard as we can. And we've decided now that we've just got to come back and look at what we've been doing for the last two years, because the whole nature of the band and the way we make music together has changed.'

Dave agreed: 'We were totally unprepared for what was going to happen. We had no way of anticipating the events that were going to take place. We were swamped by this mountain of experience, without any pause to reflect or assimilate any of it.

'This is just about the most gruelling two years that any of us have ever experienced. In a sense what happens is that you get sucked into a kind of vortex. It's not an inevitable process but it's a very difficult process to try and resist. Your natural contacts with people become distorted. You lose touch with the friends that you had. I've lost touch with maybe ninety per cent of the friends I had before the band started. That's really bad.'

At Easter, Mark and Paul went away to Brittany for a long weekend with their girlfriends. 'Mark and I were really close at the time. I think I saw Mark six nights a week for months. I don't know whether he'd worked on "Romeo And Juliet" before he went to Brittany; he probably had. It was a great house. There were lots and lots of books – Shelley, Wordsworth, Longfellow – a log fire. It was a great old house. Mark got up early one morning, made the fire and started playing his guitar. He said, "I've just written a new song, 'Romeo and Juliet'." It made me cry when I heard it because I'd become so close to Mark I knew exactly what was going on. The line where it says: "Now you just say, oh Romeo, yeah, you know I used to have a scene with him," I'd read in an interview. Those words just tore me apart. It was horrible. This guy had so much love for this girl.'

The interview referred to appeared in *Melody Maker* in January 1980. Holly Vincent is quoted as saying: 'What happened was that I had a scene with Mark Knopfler and it got to the point where he couldn't handle it and we split up, which made it impossible for Ed Bicknell to manage me as well as the Straits. It was rather an unpleasant situation.'

Paul also says: 'I could never make up my mind whether "Solid Rock" which was written on the front seat during the second US tour, was also a reference to the Holly situation. The line "You got three more fingers pointing back at you" could be the Italians, or it could be John, David and Pick.'

The band gathered at the Wood Wharf in April to begin rehearsals for the new album. According to Ed: 'It was a rather shaky group. David was recovering from his period of being ill. John had resolved his personal problems. Mark had been driving everybody loopy. Pick was pretty stable by this point.

'I can clearly remember the day I went down and they played me "Tunnel of Love" for the first time. And they played it like there were ten thousand people there. It's a very small room and it's a very intense song. It was quite loud and I was completely blown away. I thought, this is a classic. Then they played "Romeo And Juliet" and I went: Oh my God, Crikey, Wonderful. And that point is where I count the swing back.'

Dave gives another point of view: 'After *Communiqué,* I was feeling less than delighted. I just felt that the whole angle of approach was wrong. I said to Mark: "I'd like to make music that makes me feel like I used to do when I was a kid, when I was on the Octopus, being spun around. The music did something for me, combined with the feeling of being on a ride at the fair."

'I just remembered that whole thing of the Town Moor at Newcastle and the fairground there, the way you felt on a ride, and the music was playing and the association between the two things became locked into your own mind and imagination. I was basically pestering Mark to write something that worked that way. I'd like to think that was one of the reasons that he wrote "Tunnel Of Love". But I'm sure that the experience was a part of his own memory, too.'

In June the band moved to New York's Power Station to record the third album, then titled 'Tunnel of Love. Ed takes up the story: 'The studio was all set up, Jimmy was all set up, the songs were there, band ready, enthusiasm racing again. And then Jimmy introduced us to Roy Bittan, Bruce Springsteen's keyboard player, and he came to a rehearsal. He sat down and started to play, and the effect was staggering. You could feel it in the room, it lifted, it was like Concorde taking off.

'So he was there, plonking away at all that stuff. They had about five days rehearsing, and Mark had really got the bit between his teeth. They went in and cut the album, backing tracks first, as normal. Two-thirds of the way through July, it's David's turn to do his bit . . .'

What happened next is unclear. Memories differ. Mark says that Dave couldn't technically do what was asked of him, and so he sacked him. John remembers a row breaking out during the recording of 'Romeo And Juliet'. Mark, in the control box, saw Dave struggling and asked him to go back to the hotel that night and practise. The next day, Dave returned, and it was obvious that he hadn't done any practising. In the ensuing argument, Dave swore at Mark and both brothers stormed back to the hotel. Mark demanded an apology and Dave refused to give one. Finally Dave came to John to ask his advice and John told him to go home.

Paul remembers a meeting about the sleeve: 'They all came in the room, and David came in, and Mark said: "I'm not going to discuss this with him in the room until he apologises," and walked out. So David went and apologised, then he phoned me up and said: "Mark says it's not good enough."'

Dave remembers going into the studio while the band were taking a break: 'I said to the assistant engineer: "I want to try something." I was having a problem with a particular sound and I wanted to have another crack at it from another perspective.

'I started to do it, whereupon Mark came into the control room, immediately started pressing the intercom button and telling me what I was doing wasn't correct. I said: "Mark, I'm not trying to play the part." Basically, Mark was in a state that I considered to be

Reaping the rewards: Gold records for 'Sultans Of Swing' in the USA (top, presented by Jerry Wexler) and Britain

hyper-anxious, over-reacting, pressing the intercom every seven seconds and making very unhelpful remarks down the headphones. They were supposed to be having a break. I basically wanted a bit of peace and quiet to go back in and do this thing and get it out of the way.

'I said to Mark: "Why don't you take ten, take a break, go get yourself a beer or something." Because, as I saw it, this was just like someone who was blowing anxiety all over the place and generally upsetting everybody. I saw him as the problem and he saw me as the problem. Well, that was nothing new. Mark stomped out of the studio, cancelled the following day and demanded an apology, which seemed to me to be an inversion of what had been going on.'

Whatever the exact causes, Dave left the band and flew back to England. Dire Straits became a trio.

CHAPTER 6
You Get Bigger as You Go

N o one incident, no slight, perceived or intended, no single argument caused Dave Knopfler to leave. It was the culmination of a problem caused by two brothers being in the same band, the pressures of fame and staying on top, and the changing nature of the band itself.

John says: 'I think it's very rare that brothers can work together in an intense situation like that. A lot of younger brothers have a thing about their older brother, especially if they both play guitar, want to be musicians, want to be songwriters – there's bound to be conflict. But at the time it was recognized as being part of the band, so we just got on with it.'

Dave admitted the existence of a problem with Mark in the *Arena* documentary. 'It's the classic brother situation and we're just coming to terms with it now. Two years on the road has been very hard for both of us and everybody else has been in the firing line, too – Pick, John, girlfriends, Ed, Paul, road crew, everybody. It's had a spin-off effect all round. But it's for Mark and me to sort out.'

Now, Dave vehemently denies the suggestion that he was always a moaner and a complainer – at least, any more than the others – or that he was technically inadequate. But he does accept that he and Mark never did sort out their relationship.

'I left because it was no longer possible for Mark and I to work in the same band. We'd be walking around in the studio with eyes averted to the floor. We no longer had a communicating relationship, more's the pity. Sad but true. Those kind of pressures can create those kind of situations, as anyone who's been in a band knows. It's like being married to three other people. If at the end you find you want a divorce, then you have to go ahead and get one, whatever the cost.'

The structure of the band had been slowly changing, until by *Making Movies* it was no longer really a co-operative enterprise. It had become very much Mark's band, and while John and Pick (for a time) accepted that, Dave could never come to terms with it.

'We were no longer a friendly, fireside band. To me, Mark was still my brother, whereas to everyone else he was the Ayatollah. That was just a difficult transition to make. I just had a great deal of difficulty in seeing him as the Ayatollah till that day I said: "Mark why don't you just go and get a beer or something," and Paul said: "You don't tell people to do that when they're producing and making a record and you're just a musician." I'd never looked at it that way until then.'

Dave's departure eased a lot of the tension in the band, and the recording continued apace, with Sid McGinnis, who had played with (among others) Peter Gabriel and Carly Simon, drafted in on guitar.

The album, when completed, fully lived up to its intent of capturing the band's live punch on record. No longer could they be criticized for being too laid-back. The comparisons with J. J. Cale were swept away on a sea of joyous, triumphant sound. Each record Dire Straits makes has its place, and comparisons merely founder on personal value judgements, but there can be little doubt that *Making Movies* was the right sound at the right time. It fairly yelled from the rooftops: 'We're back! Just when you thought we were finished, we've returned even better than before!'

Dave: 'Mark and I no longer had a communicating relationship, more's the pity'

It's a very vibrant album, enthusiastic and positive, despite the presence of two very sad songs, 'Romeo and Juliet' and 'Hand In Hand', which, because of the strength of the arrangements, can hardly be called ballads in the conventional sense. They're contrasted with two thunderous rockers, 'Expresso Love' and 'Solid Rock', both totally unlike anything Dire Straits had previously recorded. 'Skateaway' is somewhere between the two, and 'Les Boys' is off on its own, a jokey cabaret number.

But the masterpiece is 'Tunnel Of Love', which runs through a dizzying sequence of tempi and styles, musically evoking the fairground rides which are its background.

The writing on all the songs has reached a new maturity: Mark had finally found the way to combine the 'I' of personal experience (on all songs except 'Les Boys', where he is an observer) with the detachment that makes them more than extracts from his diary. In at least one instance, 'Skateaway', this was achieved by merging two songs into one.

The most personal of the songs, 'Romeo And Juliet', is quite patently more than just Mark. It has a quality, a message, that applies to anyone who has suffered from a broken romance. In 'Tunnel Of Love', there are several different levels of meaning. Childhood fairground memories and echoes of a romance combine with a reference to the band itself: 'sing about the six-blade' referring back to 'Six Blade Knife' on the first album. There's another reference back, in 'Expresso Love', to 'Wild West End'.

After Dave left, tensions eased inside the band

And then there were three... Mark, John and Pick Withers, September 1980

The album rings with a positive attitude, a new chapter in the story of Mark Knopfler and Dire Straits, best expressed in 'Solid Rock': 'Well I'm sick of potential/I'm sick of vanity now/I'm sticking to essential reality now.'

But the reality was, there wasn't really a band, and an American tour was looming, due to start seven weeks after the completion of the album. There was a pressing need for a new guitarist (Sid McGinnis had been rejected because his manager asked for too high a fee) and also, if the songs on *Making Movies* were to be done properly, a keyboard player, possibly two.

Paul remembers: 'I know hundreds of musicians, but I couldn't think of a suitable keyboard player. Then I thought of Alan Clark. I'd met him once with Gallagher & Lyle. I'd seen him play a couple of times but I didn't really know him. I could see that he was a good player and I knew that Gallagher & Lyle had a high standard of musicianship. Also, personality-wise, he came from the right kind of background; he wasn't well-known, he wasn't a star and he wasn't working at the time.'

Mark on Pick: 'He's a very sensitive player . . . a great drummer'

John on Pick: 'To be playing with Pick was fantastic
. . . I'd never played with anyone as good as him'

Alan is another Geordie, born in March 1952 in Great Lumley, two miles south of Newcastle, the second of four children. His father passed down a musical interest. 'He was a frustrated musician, really. He used to try and play the piano, but because he was never actually shown how to do it, he never got over the initial stages of playing. But he was a part-time singer. He'd get up in pubs, just as a means of enjoying himself.'

His father was also quick to spot a potential musical talent. 'When I was about six or seven, my parents caught me plonking on the piano and I was immediately whisked off to lessons. That drove any inclination to play the piano completely out of me.'

But the musical bug struck again: 'I started getting interested again when I had my appendix removed, when I was about thirteen or fourteen. I was off school for three or four weeks, and after that I just started playing.'

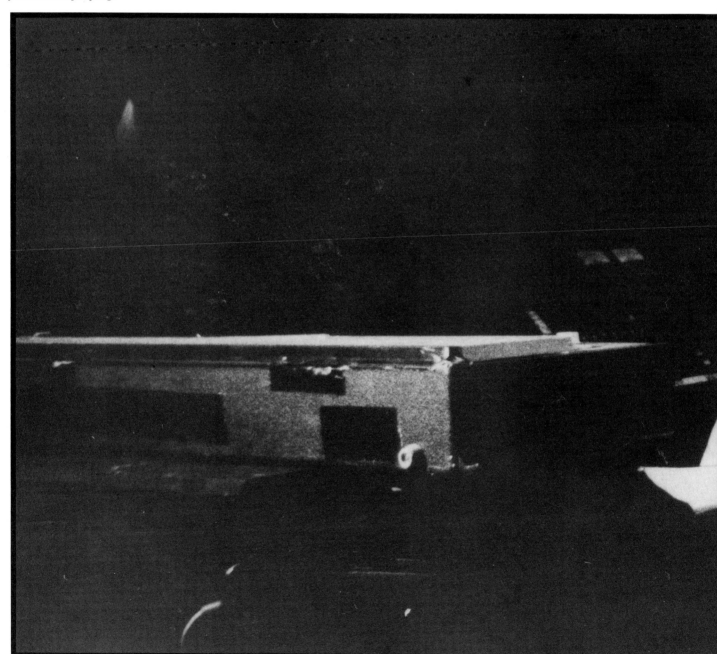

Alan took formal lessons and had soon learned enough to play in working men's clubs. 'They were a boon for keyboard players who wanted to make a living. I used to play a Hammond organ, using bass pedals and stuff, working with a drummer. I started doing freelance when I was fourteen, then, when I was about sixteen, I played for about a year and a half in one club. You had to be able to sight read music, and the scene was that we'd play a few tunes before the featured artist came along. I played with Matt Monro, the Bachelors, P.J. Proby. I remember him particularly. He had two bottles of brandy before he went on-stage. He sang "Somewhere" a bar behind us, right throught the entire song.

'Scattered through all these cabaret acts would be all these sixties bands: Dave Dee, Dozy, Beaky, Mick and Tich; the Merseybeats; Del Shannon. Even at the time I used to consider it as I do now: pretty ridiculous. It was totally uninspiring. I can think of better musical

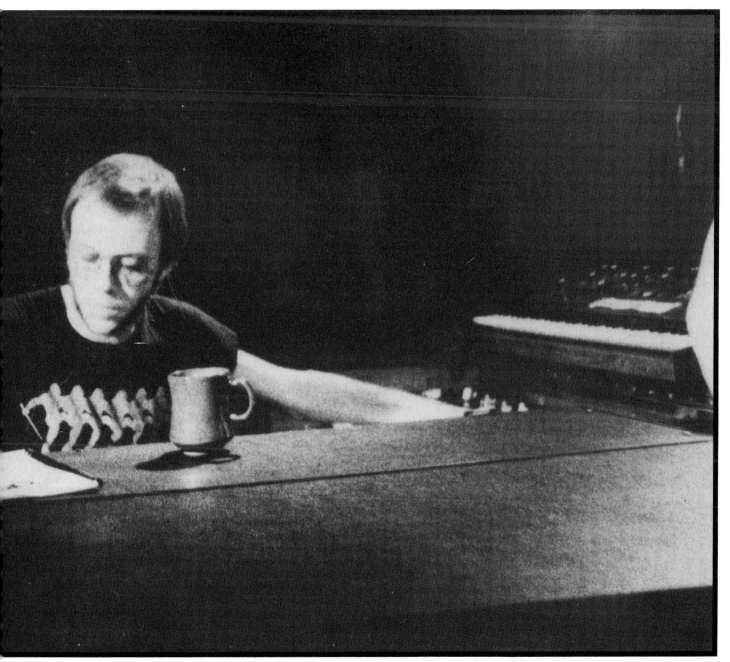

Alan Clark: 'I came down for the audition and never went back'

Alan's keyboards added a new dimension to the Straits sound

apprenticeships to go through. But it was profitable. By the time I was sixteen I had a car and was earning twice as much as my father.'

It carried him through Chester-le-Street Grammar to Durham Technical College, where he mainly studied music, and was accepted for the Guildhall School of Music. But work was plentiful, and Alan felt no compulsion to head south towards a possible career as a music teacher.

'I just left technical college. At the time I was working in the Carousel Club in Chester-le-Street, which was the last of the casino clubs. The cabarets played for a week there – definitely a step up from the one-night jobs. Shortly after that I went and worked on cruise ships in the Caribbean for several months, and I spent about eighteen months based in Miami. Then I came back and just carried on working the night clubs. I suppose in a lot of ways I'm a late developer. I spent most of my youth chasing after girls.'

On his return home there was a nagging feeling that he ought to be playing in bands. 'But basically there weren't any bands around who I wanted to play with. I just felt this need to associate myself more with bands than cabaret work. I played with a few local musicians who had bands – including a re-formed Geordie with Brian Johnston, who's now in AC/DC – but basically they were absolutely dreadful.'

Then he was offered a job with Splinter, a much-heralded signing to George Harrison's Dark Horse label, but now slowly fading in popularity after their only hit, 'Costafine Town', in 1974.

'I decided I was going to make a serious shot at it. That was basically the start of my musical career as far as I'm concerned, because up until that point I wasn't really trying to get anywhere. So I started practising seriously. Splinter were a lot more musically inclined than a lot of bands I'd worked with in the past. It was a lot more satisfying for me to work with them.'

Splinter gave Alan a grounding in the rock 'n' roll way of life: a European tour supporting Gregg Allman and Cher; radio sessions; recording an (unreleased) album; dates in Japan. And during the three years he spent with them, he made the first serious attempt to create his own music.

'Splinter's manager suggested I get a few demos together, so I linked up with a singer called Jimmy Lowry. I wrote most of the parts of the songs, and then there were a few instrumental pieces. It started out as a serious venture, but we ended up making the same mistake as everyone else, trying to come up with a hit single. It got a fair bit of interest, but really it was grasping at straws to get something happening.'

Alan joined Gallagher & Lyle for a while, and later spent a summer touring festivals with Lindisfarne.

'Then I was just lying in bed one morning and the phone rang. It was Paul Cummins. He asked me what I was doing – nothing – and then asked whether there was a chance I might play with Dire Straits. I'd heard the band back at the beginning. A friend of mine bought the first album, and of course there were all the references to Newcastle, so he hammered it into me. I must say that I didn't take that much of an interest in it, because it was all guitar. But I still liked it.

'Anyway, a couple of weeks after the call I went down to London, to the Wood Wharf, and never came back. They'd said to just prepare for a couple of days at the most, but after that time they said: "You've got the job."'

Paul continues: 'And then we needed a guitarist. I turned down one guy, and Hal phoned up, so I thought we'd give him a try, rather than have the band sitting around doing nothing.'

Hal comes from California, though his parents are Russian. His father was born in Leningrad, his mother in Odessa. They met when they were deported by the Nazis to work-camps in Germany. After the war they married and emigrated to America, first living in New York and then Monterey, where Hal was born in June 1953.

'As far back as I can remember, I always had this thing about the guitar. When I was about five my parents bought me this plastic white guitar. It was really a toy – it had pictures of cowboys on it. I had that for ages and I could never get it to work; it always sounded terrible. A few years later someone older came over and told me that it had five top E strings and one bottom E.'

More formal musical training came later, when the family moved to Washington DC. 'When I was about nine years old, I started studying piano for a couple of years. I was actually learning how to read music, but I didn't like it very much. I think it was probably because of the teachers I had, though I was more interested in actually being able to do something right away, as opposed to having to go through the whole regimented thing of learning scales and notes, so I got really bored. I liked the idea of the guitar because you could learn chords pretty quickly.

'Then the Beatles came out, and when I started to listen to them and the Stones, I said: "This is it! I've got to learn how to play guitar."'

That came on a holiday to a Delaware beach resort, where a family friend spent the whole time teaching Hal to play well enough for him to convince his parents that he was serious. They bought him a cheap acoustic guitar for $19.95, but insisted that he take lessons.

'I hated the teacher. He was a big fat guy who owned the music store and he was really greasy and slimy. After one gruelling lesson he turned round to me and said: "You'll never make a guitar player." And this was at the age of eleven!'

But at school there were others eager to play, and a band was formed for a school talent show – H.A. and the Lindells. With a borrowed black Dan Electro and a twee Fender Champ for an amp, Hal made his public debut performing the Beatles' 'All My Loving'. Waiting at home for him that night was a brand new Kent electric, a present from his mother and father, especially for the repeat of the talent show in front of parents. Out stepped H.A. and the Lindells, Hal struck up the opening chords of 'All My Loving', and then – disaster. Everyone was singing half a step higher than the guitar. 'And that's when I first discovered that you can actually tune guitars.'

When he moved to Junior High School, Hal joined another band, the Nightriders, who would set up in the cafeteria after school and play for anyone who wanted to listen, five or six songs a set. 'There were a lot of greasers around, so if you didn't play soul music you used to get beat up.' The repertoire was mainly Atlantic, Stax and Motown: Sam and Dave, Eddie Floyd's 'Knock On Wood', Wilson Pickett's 'In The Midnight Hour', instrumentals like 'Twine Time' and James Brown's 'Night Train' were all there, along with a peppering of current hits like 'Louie Louie' and 'Hang On Sloopy'.

Moving on to High School, Hal found another band, Sudden Rush, but the Sudden was later dropped. 'It was my first serious band – we actually had a PA system. Basically, that's where I really started learning to play. We'd do local colleges and universities – I think my

Hal Lindes at a rehearsal in the autumn of 1980

sister got us our first gig, at her fraternity house at the University of Maryland.

'We'd do four half-hour sets with a break. It was cover music – Beatles, Stones, Chuck Berry, English stuff. That meant a lot of songs, so we'd do everything twice and improvise – put in a long solo. I remember we did "Feelin' Alright", the Traffic number. You could make that last for a week, with really long, extended solos.'

Rush lasted through a reluctant move to university. 'There were parental pressures, and at that particular time I couldn't really offer any alternatives, so I agreed to try it. And I did – for one semester.' Rush started taking up more and more time. There were personnel changes and the band started playing further afield: up to Pennsylvania and Delaware, anywhere there were gigs. Inevitably, studies were abandoned and Hal dropped out of university.

Another obsession took over. He wanted to come to England, partly because the music had been such an inspiration, partly because growing up in a European environment in America had made him curious to see what it was like on the other side of the Atlantic.

'I saved up the money and one day I told my parents that I was going to England. They didn't take it very seriously. So I just got on a plane and came. I checked into a little hotel, a bed and breakfast place off Kensington High Street. I started meeting people right away. Initially I was just going to hang out for a while, but some people helped me find a flat . . .'

Flipping through *Melody Maker* Hal spotted an ad for a guitarist. It was with a pub band called Yellow Bird. Hal joined up and set off on the London pub circuit, before helping set up a new band, Darling. They had a millionaire for a manager, a record deal with Charisma, which produced one album, *Put It Down To Experience,* and lots of gigs. But Hal has unhappy memories.

'It just didn't turn out the way I thought it was going to. When we were sitting around each other's flats trying to get material together, it was fine, but as soon as we got a manager, everyone's attitude in the band changed. And not for the better.

'It was a real eye-opener. It was my first exposure to business, because most musicians who aren't successful don't realize that there's a big business behind it. Eventually I felt I'd had enough of going up and down the motorway and not really getting any satisfaction out of it, so I split.'

On his own at home, Hal spent six months writing songs, trying to discover whether he had any potential. And then a fluke put him in touch with Al Kooper, whose career spanned doo-wop with the Royal Teens, Dylan's breakthrough into electric music, and jazz-rock with Blood, Sweat and Tears. He was now a noted producer. Kooper listened, liked what he heard and decided to produce Hal's songs.

Then, by another coincidence, Hal heard that Dire Straits were looking for a guitarist. 'I really liked the Straits, so I thought: That sounds interesting. I spoke to Paul Cummins and he asked me what I'd done, who I liked, what kind of guitar I was playing. I told him a Strat, and I think that gave me a few points. I asked him whether there were any songs I should know, because I knew no Straits songs apart from what I'd heard on record. I had no idea of how they were constructed.

'So he gave me four songs, three of which were on *Communiqué,*

Hal: not just a pretty face – he cut his teeth in high school bands

which I didn't have. I put down the phone – this was about nine or ten at night – and started ringing everyone I knew, trying to get hold of *Communiqué*. I finally got hold of it and sat up all night, listening to the songs.'

The next day Hal drove down to the Wood Wharf and strolled in, white '59 Strat under his arm. Paul says: 'I was fuming because he was half an hour late. But as soon as he walked in the room, Mark and I looked at each other, and nodded.' Mark handed Hal a Walkman and said: 'Listen to this. Don't try to figure out the chords; just listen to it and get the feel, that's all.'

Hal remembers the day well. 'It was "Tunnel Of Love", which is like a hundred hours long. The first thing I'm trying to do is work out the chords so I could play the thing. I listened to it three times and I thought, Hey, this could be really good, because at the time my playing was more like rock, more aggressive, which was the way *Making Movies* was going.'

'Right,' said Mark. 'Let's plug in the guitars and we'll go through it.' Strapping on his Sunburst Schecter (a favourite, which was later stolen), Mark went into the opening riff of 'Tunnel Of Love', showing Hal the chording of the parts he'd have to play.

'There was an obvious lead line that runs throughout the song, and Mark was going to have to do it, so the other parts were going to have to be covered. What he does is, he'll start off playing the lead lines and then halfway through he'll break off and start playing fiddly, semi-lead lines. He'd just turn round to me and say: "Right, do this." He showed me exactly what he wanted me to do, and I just basically tried to do the best that I could.

'Obviously, from the beginning, I had a lot of work to do on the guitar. Mark's so stylized in his playing. You couldn't just take a normal block chord and put it behind him because it would jar; it would be like trying to fit a square peg into a round hole. So I had to do quite a bit of refining in my playing, almost like taking a piece of sandpaper to it and smoothing off the edges. Basically, I was more of a rock 'n' roll guitarist, in the Keith Richards mould. I was pretty much into plugging the guitar into a Hi-Watt, turning it up to eight and letting the speakers and amp wail.'

Meanwhile, Alan had been establishing a crucial role for himself in the band. Not only were there new songs to be learned, but old ones had to be adapted for keyboards. 'I'd get back to John's house, where I was staying, at about nine after rehearsal, and I'd sit up for a couple of hours and listen to the next song. Then I'd write out the piano part, note for note. It was a great way of learning what people have played. And of course, the next day I'd go and put the music out and play it immediately, which got the momentum going for the entire song.

'It was like a combination of me and Mark working out the keyboard parts. He might have a conception for a few lines of what the keyboards should do, and then I'd be musing through something and he'd say: "Fine. Use it." It worked very well, because Mark was very open-minded about it, and he was very keyboard-orientated.'

It was finally decided that one keyboard player would suffice, and after a few short weeks of rehearsal a new, invigorated Dire Straits were sitting in a phone-booth dressing-room in a small club in Vancouver, Canada, listening to the records booming through the walls.

For Hal, at least, it was a nervy occasion. 'They made the

'I didn't know how people would react to me replacing David'

announcement: "Ladies and Gentlemen, will you please put your hands together for Dire Straits!" and the old heart's like thumping a mile a minute and I'm asking myself: What am I *doing* here?

'One of the reasons I was nervous was that not knowing all that much about the Straits, I didn't know how people would react to me replacing David. I didn't know whether there would be any resentment, like: "Who's this guy? Where's David?" But then, when we walked on-stage, everyone seemed really glad to see us.

'So we started off on "Once Upon A Time In The West". Alan did his whistle on the Prophet and just as I hit the first D, the string went "boing!" and flew off into the audience, Mark must have thought, Oh God, what have we got here? but he just looked over at me and smiled . . .'

But it was a good gig, a fine start and Dire Straits began moving down the West Coast of North America, playing clubs all the way. San Francisco was surreal. They played to a typically laid-back audience, stuffed with food, drink and drugs. But sitting back, waiting to be impressed, they didn't really get into the show, which was rather unnerving. Back at the hotel, situated in an outrageously gay section of town, Hal woke up the next morning to see a dummy, like Guy Fawkes, hanging from a noose outside his window.

But the music was coming together so well, it could only be taken as a good omen.

CHAPTER 7

City of Night...
City of Light

Los Angeles is a strange place, a city with an image, a showpiece with a lot to live up to but nothing to back it up. Home of the stars, home of the American record industry, and yet there are no homes visible: just houses, motels, factories, shops, offices, apartment complexes. Nothing looks more than twenty years old, and it's sprawled out further than the eye can see. It's an impersonal city, to the outsider, at least; a town with no core. Take away the suburbs, with their names redolent of the movies, and what's left is nothing.

There are cities within cities here – Culver City, Temple City, Universal City – as though the whole sprawling mass has been assembled by a child adding bits on to a basic Lego set. The distances involved are great; the automobile rules. White Rolls Royces rub fenders with rusting heaps of Detroit junk, flash Caddies tower over tiny Minis. In a weird reversal of roles, only the wealthy can afford the economic European models; the ordinary Joe is stuck with the chrome monsters and their gross appetite for ever-more-expensive gas.

'One giant parking lot,' is John's verdict on Los Angeles.

The Straits have hired cars for the first leg of the US tour, and they drive down the Coast Highway into LA past Malibu, beach resort of the ultra-rich, and then hit the legendary Sunset Boulevard. Detouring through Bel-Air to view the architectural Disneyland built to satisfy the grandiose fantasies and gigantic egos of generations of movie stars, they rejoin Sunset at its tacky end, flashing past seedy stripshows ('Guaranteed totally nude or your money back. Amateur night Sunday') and dodgy nightclubs ('Miss Pat Collins, the hip hypnotist'), all overlooked by giant billboards begging attention for the latest star, film, record or show. Tucked in amongst all this is the unprepossessing Roxy Club. It's Tuesday, 28 October 1980. The

Cruisin': Dire Straits reach Los Angeles

temperature is eighty-two degrees, and tonight and tomorrow, the sign relays, Dire Straits are sold out.

A couple of hundred yards further on, down a side street, is the Sunset Marquis, a cool, elegant, discreet hotel much favoured by touring bands. Check in, a meal, a rest, and off to the Roxy for the inevitable sound check.

There are problems with the tickets. In a club seating just 500, 150 seats have been taken by Warners. Record company personnel are not reckoned to be the most receptive of audiences, and there will be plenty of industry figures here tonight. 'They don't applaud here,' says Mark. 'They just rattle their silver coke spoons.'

Ryan O'Neal and Farrah Fawcett call up for separate tables (who do they think they're fooling?) while outside, two dedicated fans are already queuing, sleeping-bags and Thermos flasks beside them, for the next night's show. Delighted at the prospect of having at least two genuine fans in the audience, Mark insists they're given reservations for a decent table and saves them a pavement vigil.

In a town where the movies have elevated the gangster to the figure of super-hero, it seems almost fitting that Ed should be being pursued by a mysterious figure threatening to break his arms unless he's paid 5,000 dollars, an imaginary debt stretching back to a Talking Heads gig years ago.

'Don't fucking worry,' says a helpful American friend who looks like he's just stepped off a Hollywood lot. 'I'll bury him.' Deep swallows. This guy really *means* it. 'Can't you just persuade him to *back off* a little?' asks Paul. No problem.

After this drama, the show itself is bound to be an anti-climax, and indeed the verdict in the dressing-room afterwards is not good. There's been a problem with the sound cutting out mid-song, eventually traced to the power source, which is the same for lights and sound, and woefully inadequate. A generator truck is hired for the next night to boost up the power.

As if that weren't enough, the stage air-conditioner was switched on halfway through, freezing sweat on the musicians' bodies. That's a quick way to catch pneumonia.

Still, the grins and smiles have to be moulded on faces as the Straits prepare to meet the liggers, a sprinkling of stars (their benefit night is tomorrow), and the inevitable cast of record company salesmen, all of whom want to shake hands with the band, and claim to have broken their record in various unlikely-sounding places.

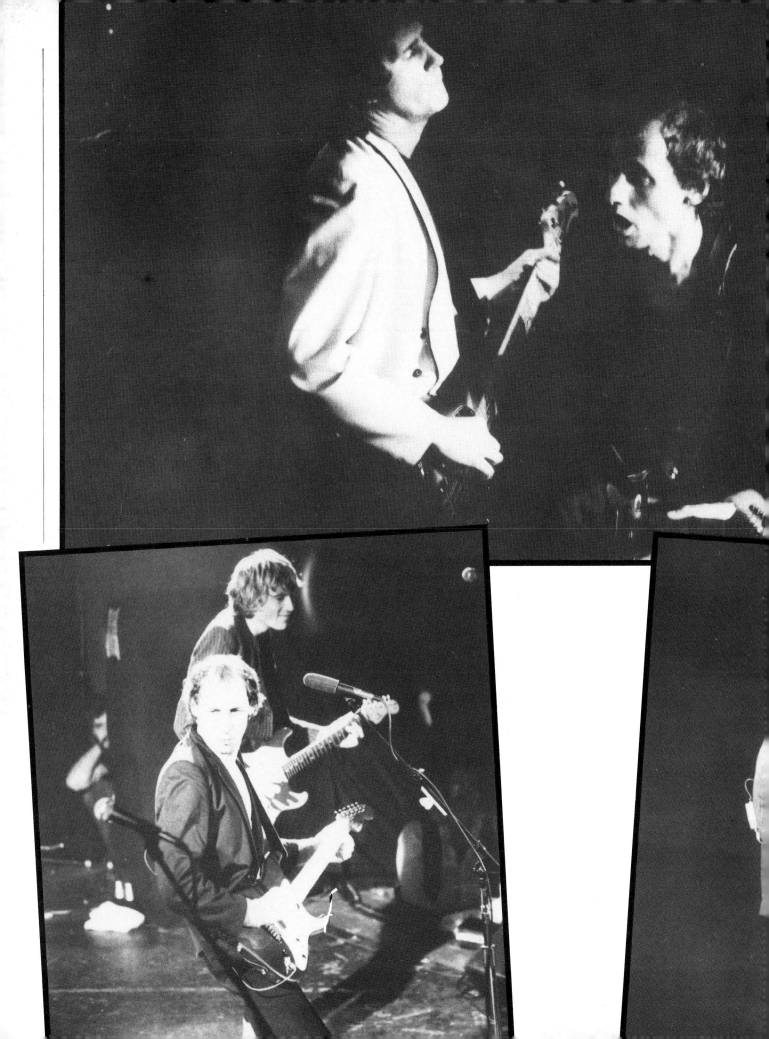

The Roxy, Los Angeles: 'They don't applaud here . . . they just rattle their silver coke spoons'

109

Solid Gold Straits: appearing on TV in the States

Good timing: rehearsing 'Skateaway' for a TV show

They give a twenty-minute lecture on the problems of rack-jobbing in the Midwest. The band back out of the door, heading for the hotel, glad-handing all the way.

Wednesday. A hole has been found in the schedule, and Ed's filled it. So it's up early for the drive round to TV station KTLA where they will tape two songs, 'Sultans' and 'Skateaway' (the American single from *Communiqué*), for a show called *Solid Gold*.

They're only miming, but the session drags on and on. The band are left hanging about on the set while the director adjusts his camera angles and copes with a host of technical difficulties, forced to listen to the blatherings of a so-called comic who's supposed to be keeping the audience happy.

'If you're wondering what the smoke is,' he says pointing to the dry ice curling around the stage, 'it's a couple of midgets smoking marijuana.' Hilarious, but completely lost on the audience, whose average age appears to be sixty-five. The major problem in LA is finding enough people to make up a live audience. There are so many TV shows taped each day, scalphunters are paid two dollars a head to round up those too feeble to run away.

There's scarcely time to eat before it's back to the Roxy for the sound check; this evening they're precisely timing a version of 'Skateaway' which will be performed live on another TV show, *Fridays*, in two days' time.

Showtime. And tonight it goes like a dream. Old songs and new songs mesh into a flowing sea of memorable music. 'Once Upon A Time In The West', taut and tense . . . 'News', brooding and menacing under Pick's metronomic drumming . . . 'Sultans', whirling away in celebration. And there's a surprise. Up steps Roy Bittan, in LA with Bruce Springsteen for shows across town, to recreate the keyboard part on 'Tunnel Of Love' he played on the recording. Uproar. Pandemonium. Encores. 'Wild West End' and 'Where Do You Think You're Going' see Dire Straits quietly off-stage.

Just before the set started, Bob Dylan had discreetly slipped in, and now he's backstage, waiting for the Straits to wipe off the sweat and fling open the doors to superstars, semi-stars, record company executives, promo men, and a loonie girl who's earholing everyone she meets about a rock opera she's just written. Sure, Bob enjoyed the show, being much taken with the lights, and soon he's deep in conversation with Mark.

The party thins out, the floating cast of back-slappers and well-wishers moving on to intimate restaurants and select nightspots. Someone's heard that Robert Redford's in town and, yeah, it'd be good to see ol' Bob again. There's this little property he might be interested in . . .

A hardcore of musicians and hangers-on moves over to Mark's room at the hotel. Dylan settles into a plush armchair and engages Pick in deep conversation. Then he disappears into a bedroom with bassist Tim Drummond and a black girl singer. Paul Cummins is despatched to collect two Ovation acoustic guitars.

'Bob's going to have a sing-song,' Paul announces to a largely unimpressed room. These suave and supercool LA folk carry on their conversations, oblivious to the music that's seeping out from the bedroom. Occasionally the curious wander in to be confronted by Bob perched in the centre of the bed, his singer sitting crosslegged on the pillows, Tim Drummond hunched over the other guitar on the carpet.

The songs are new, never recorded, sweet, sweet melodies and beautiful harmonies, the crystal Gospel clarity of the girl's voice soaring high over Dylan's familiar nasal tones. A long jam on the old blues classic, 'Baby What You Want Me To Do', draws Mark into the room. Taking the acoustic proffered by Tim, Mark and Bob start little dancing runs on their guitars, instrumentals that discover a tune as if independent of the fingers on the strings.

By now, the small bedroom is getting crowded. Mark persuades a reluctant Bob to move into the lounge. Perched on the edge of a chair, he sits facing Mark and performs song after song, no titles, no frills, just voice and guitar sprinkling musical magic through the room. One song, 'Woman At The Well', with those haunting vocal harmonies between Dylan and his companion, leads into a bluesy instrumental with Mark taking the lead.

'That's a good tune, Bob,' says Mark, when they've played it to the end.

'Yeah. What is it?'

'I thought it was one of yours.'

'No, it's not my tune. I thought it was yours.'

It was in the air, that night.

A Gospel-sounding number from Bob, 'Ain't No Man Righteous Enough', to the accompaniment of a sacrilegious whoop from Pick, and then Mark's urging Bob to try more familiar favourites from his back pages.

'We do a lot of old tunes now,' says Bob. 'Yeah, let's see, we do "Fever".' Mark strikes up the chords, but Bob lets it fizzle out.

'Do that one that goes "Guns across the prairie",' says Mark, but Bob will not be drawn into the past.

'Here's a tune you might like,' he says, and goes into a jokey song, 'A Couple More Years,' which draws nervous laughter from the audience, barely daring to move a muscle in so intense an atmosphere. The tension is dissipated with another light number, 'She's Not For You'.

The next song lasts only half a verse before Dylan falters on the words.

'Having trouble with my lyrics tonight, Mark.'

'You always did write too many, Bob'.

Songs are started and never finished, tunes are dug out of memories shared and personal, and all too soon it's 3 a.m. Time for musicians to get some rest, and for audience to dance home on air.

The next day, John, Alan, Pick and Hal are still glowing, scarcely believing that they'd seen two master musicians playing music for themselves in circumstances that will probably never be repeated, a little bit of history enacted before their eyes and ears.

Only Ed is keeping his cool: 'The thing about stars is, they're only people like the rest of us. They all have to get up in the morning and take a shit.' But he was impressed. We all were.

A couple of days later, Dire Straits headed off for Dallas, the next stage on the tour that took them through the South and up the

Smile – you're on TV! Watching a playback of *Fridays* at the studios

East Coast, sticking in clubs until they hit New York, where they
played theatres, winding up at the Massey Hall in Toronto, Canada
on 23 November.

Meanwhile, *Making Movies* had re-established them critically
and commercially. To date it has sold 3.3 million copies worldwide.
And back in England, there was another surprise: the single,
'Romeo And Juliet', was taking off.

Ed says: 'The very first thing we did with Hal and Alan was a
taping of that song for *Multi-Coloured Swap Shop,* the BBC's
Saturday morning kid's show. There were quite a lot of BBC people
there who said: "Oh, what a wonderful song. If you put that out, we'll
play it." So we said we would, because originally "Solid Rock" was
being touted as the single choice. But it wasn't really representative
of the record it was on; *Making Movies* is essentially the first side.

'Phonogram really wanted "Romeo And Juliet" more than the
band, who, I think, thought they'd never get this away. And in fact it
outsold "Sultans". It was very important in another way, in that it got
rid of the albatross that "Sultans" had become, and showed that the
band had breadth and variety. There had been a comment, perhaps
not totally unjustified, that everything that had followed it sounded
like "Sultans". "Lady Writer" wasn't that dissimilar.'

British dates started in December, and the band carried on
around the world until July 1981. Ireland, Italy, Spain, Australia, New
Zealand, Germany, Denmark, Sweden, Norway, Finland, France,
Switzerland, Italy (second time around), Belgium and Luxembourg:
all gave the Straits an ecstatic welcome.

Hal is still high on it. 'The British tour was bigger places than
America; there was a big production, with the lights, and it was
starting to feel good. And then by the time we got to Ireland, it was
really starting to kick and the audiences were incredibly
responsive. You could just feel that the band had gone up another
rung. By the time we got to Australia, the band was *really* kicking. In
New Zealand we did an outdoor gig in front of twenty thousand
people, which is the most people I'd ever played for before.

Left: More trophies for the mantelpiece: the band with tour manager Paul Cummins
Below: Travelling band. Musicians, crew and management in Europe, 1981

Left: More trophies for the mantelpiece: the band with tour manager Paul Cummins

Below: Travelling band. Musicians, crew and management in Europe, 1981

'I work totally off the audience, because if it's a duff gig, a duff audience, you have to try and create something that's not there. In Switzerland, where I thought the audience would be really reserved, they went bananas. They were whistling and screaming, louder and louder. They were producing more decibels than we were with our entire amplification. They were deafening us on-stage.

'When you look out in a hall and it's packed solid, say twelve thousand people, so the only way they can applaud is by putting their hands over their heads, you see this sea of hands and the bodies are all swaying. A lot of atmosphere, a lot of electricity gets generated, and I just go with it.'

Making Movies made its biggest impact in Italy, where it sold 600,000 copies (by comparison, the album sold 500,000 in America, which, in its way, was excellent without a hit single) and the single 'Tunnel Of Love' became a huge hit. When the band came to Turin to play in front of 90,000 people at the football ground, their fame had reached Beatles-like proportions.

Alan smiles. 'I got a bit over-confident about not being recognized. I went for a walk around the stadium, and there were all these stalls selling bootleg T-shirts, some of which were absolutely horrific. Someone had tried to do a drawing of Mark from a picture in a magazine, and he had severely receding hair, terrible gaps in his teeth, lines under his eyes and a little crown on his head. Underneath was written *Sultans Of Swim*. Obviously they'd had a little trouble with the language.

'So anyway, I came out of one of the entrances and got about halfway around the ground when I heard this little female voice shout: "Alan!" and before I knew it I was surrounded by adolescent females. I had to walk back, saying: "Shhh, shhh, keep it to yourself," otherwise I'd have been mobbed.'

Ed's verdict on the whole tour was that it re-established Dire Straits after the hiccup of *Communiqué*. 'The band was incomparably better than before, it was like a proper group. I wondered how we ever got anywhere with the first line-up. Some people regret the passing of the shuffle rockaboogie, but you have to move on.

'And the group was pretty happy within itself, although Pick was obviously less happy than the others. Hal and Alan, from their point of view, had come up really from obscurity and, for one of the cheapest wages ever paid, had found true happiness. Mark and John were really gee-ed up; Mark was really chuffed. *Making Movies* had got the closest that he'd wanted to get on record at that point.

'He'd become much more prominent. It wasn't really the democratic group it once had been. It's a very subtle thing. He doesn't come in and dictate; it's not like having an arranger who's written out dots. But he has a pretty close idea of how he wants the song to appear and sound. So when we finished the world tour and got off at Luxembourg, everyone went "uhhh". But it was a smiling sort of "uhhh".'

A long rest was obviously overdue, and the band went back to their respective homes and families. In the interim, Ed wrote to about a dozen British film producers, sent them a cassette of *Making Movies,* drew their attention to the success of Dire Straits, and said that Mark was interested in doing a film score.

'We'd had a couple of abortive attempts at getting this together

Above: 'And the big wheel kept on turning'
Left: 'A long time ago came a man on a track . . .' Mark and Alan working on 'Telegraph Road'

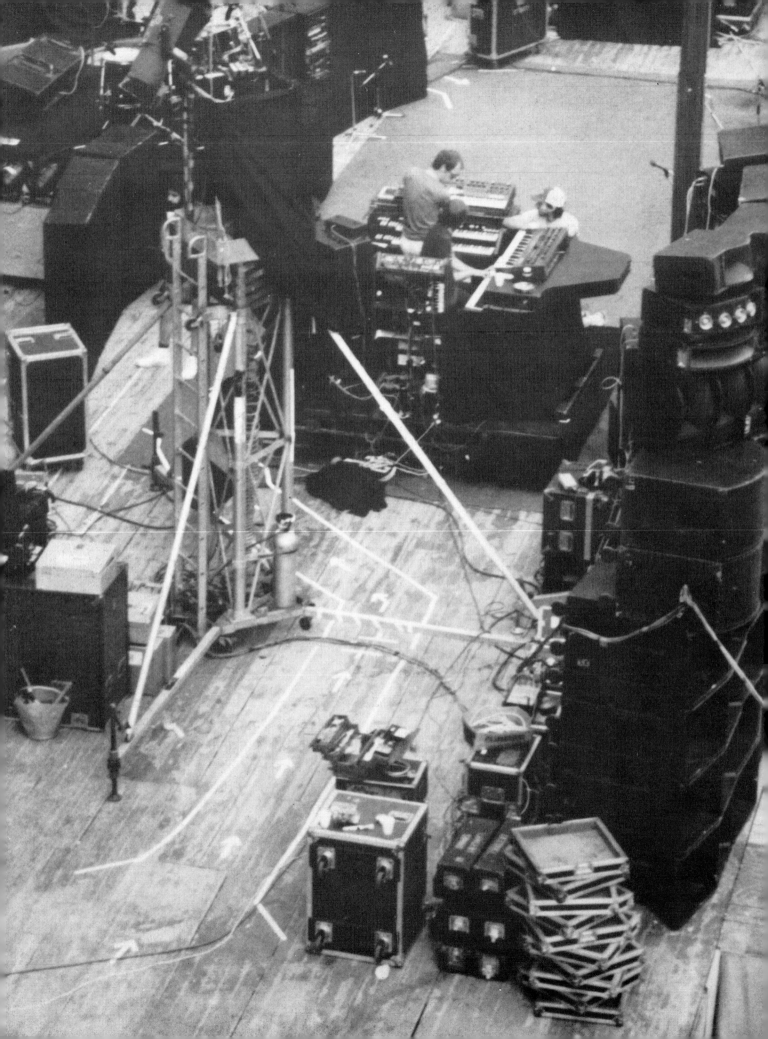

Previous pages: Wired for sound – the band's PA dwarfs the musicians

before. Representatives of large American studios had met me for breakfast at Ben Frank's, on Sunset Strip, and suggested films that Robert Redford would produce. When asked whether Robert Redford knew anything about this, they'd say: "Well, no. Not yet. But he will." That type of approach.'

Ed received three replies from the British producers. Mark Shivas was making a film about Maria Callas, which was obviously unsuitable. Don Boyd offered *An Unsuitable Job For A Woman,* a mystery thriller which was rejected after a viewing as no one could figure out the mystery or the thrills. But the most promising reply came from David Puttnam, who had Bill Forsyth's script for *Local Hero.* Forsyth, whose movie *Gregory's Girl* was about to

Home again: Britain gets its first look at the new five-piece Straits, December 1980

become a big hit, would direct, and Puttnam, also destined to have a smash on his hands with *Chariots Of Fire,* would produce.

Ed read through the script, liked it, and sent it to Mark in New York. He called back: 'This is great. Tell me about it.'

Ed says: 'We got involved before actors and crew had been cast. I give David Puttnam every credit for the fact that he took a chance, because Mark had never done a film score. It turns out that David's son is a mad Straits fan and David is obsessed with the guitar playout of "Tunnel Of Love". He thought that if Mark could recapture the emotional effect of that, then he'd be right for the type of thing Bill was trying to create with the film.'

Inevitably, the film schedule was put back, so in January 1982 Mark called the band together. They booked into the Wood Wharf to rehearse for a new album. It had been a prolific songwriting period. 'Telegraph Road' had already appeared in live shows from Australia on, but there were twenty other songs. Mark wanted to make a double album, much to Ed's horror.

'It's great to be working in music and not in car parts, but you do sometimes have to take a commercial view as well. A double album would have been difficult. I would have had huge problems with the record companies and the price of it would have made it a problematical item to sell.'

Economic reason prevailed, and *Love Over Gold,* became a single album. The band flew off to New York on 1 March and recorded seven songs, two of which, 'The Way It Always Starts' and 'Private Dancer', were not used. ('The Way It Always Starts' was re-recorded with vocals by Gerry Rafferty for *Local Hero.*) Another new song, 'Posters, Badges, Stickers And T-Shirts', an ironic comment on merchandizing, became the B-side of the 'Private Investigations' single.) By now, Mark felt confident enough to produce himself, with the help of engineer Neil Dorfsman.

Love Over Gold was another step forward; only five songs, each at least six minutes long, headed by the fourteen-and-a-half-minute 'Telegraph Road'. By now the mixture of personal experience and broader themes had been folded in so thoroughly that it was no longer possible to pinpoint one actual incident that the songs were about. The 'I' character was both a participant and a detached observer. Musically, the songs range from the epic construction of 'Telegraph Road', changes of pace and style sweeping the song ever upward to a climax, to the jauntiness of 'Industrial Disease', really the odd man out on an album that's sombre and serious and rich in melodic invention.

'Telegraph Road' was originally inspired by an actual street in Detroit that the band visited during that disastrous second US tour. Mark explains: 'The song is just a combination of circumstances. I was sitting there on the bus and this road seemed to be going on forever. The motor industry was really run-down then. I was reading this *Growth Of The Soil* book, and the song is a combination of the book and the place I was at.

'It's a bit movie-esque, for want of a better word. There are long-shots, and we'd talk about the middle instrumental section as the movie section, because you'd feel that the camera would pull away and you would get a view of things as they were and as they are now. It's like a film, with its own people and little trains and trucks, a lake and fields and buildings. I'm not massively fond of it, but there it is. It just got done.'

128

Marking time: the *Love Over Gold* sessions at the Power Station, New York, March–June 1982

The moody atmosphere of 'Private Investigations', redolent of forties and fifties Hollywood film noir, developed out of the way the band performed 'News' on-stage, with the drum pulsebeat accentuated.

'I think that "Private Investigations" is partly about writing songs. It was sparked off by something that I'd read about Philip Marlowe. Basically he's on the side of right, but, generally speaking, up against it and trying to do something positive in an extremely bitter environment. Chandler's world was LA, which always was kind of bleak.

'The song is a little bit tongue-in-cheek. It's amusing. You hear different interpretations of it, but to me it's deliberately movie. A little soundtrack, really. I don't think it's any big deal. It's just what was there. It's not intended to mystify people.

'I had this Italian-style movie tune. I was playing acoustic guitars because I wasn't working with the band at the time. And I had a movie score coming up, so I was doing that kind of thing anyway. I had this other instrumental piece and they were both in the same key. They just went together well.'

The complete musician: Mark's guitars (below) – but he works out on the piano

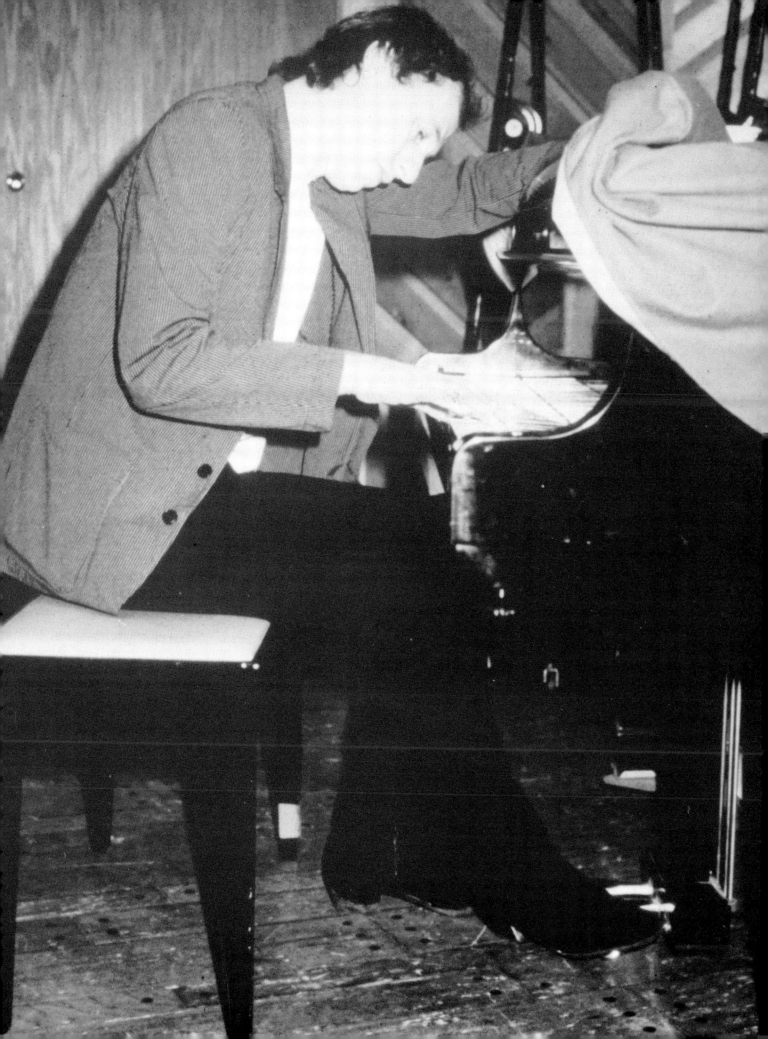

Mark recording *Love Over Gold*: 'The album is a bit heavy-duty'

Mark maintains that 'It Never Rains' started as a doodle and has nothing to do with anything else, yet along with 'Romeo And Juliet' and 'Love Over Gold', it appears to form a trilogy about a single affair. On 'Romeo And Juliet' the man is an incurable romantic, dumbstruck that his Juliet should desert him for another. 'It Never Rains' refers to 'your new Romeo' and is quite clearly about a girl musician, for whom, now that she has fallen on hard times, there is no sympathy: 'You never gave a damn about who you pick up/And leave lying bleeding on the ground/You screw people over on the way up/Because you thought that you were never coming down'. By 'Love Over Gold' there is an acceptance of the reality of what has happened.

The album was completed by early June, by which time shooting had already started on *Local Hero*. The plot of the film is fairly

134

simple: a giant American petro-chemical corporation plans to build an oil-refining plant in a remote Scottish fishing village. A young executive is despatched from Texas, and together with the company's Scottish representative, tries to buy up the land.

The two oilmen get drawn into the easy-going lifestyle; meanwhile, the villagers get more and more excited at the prospect of making their fortunes and retiring in comfort. Then, at the last minute, opposition comes from an unlikely source, and the chairman of the oil corporation, played by Burt Lancaster, arrives to sort things out – with surprising results.

It's a gentle film with no bad guys, only ordinary human beings with the usual weaknesses. For Mark, it presented a challenge in the sheer breadth of style that was called for by the script – from trucking Texas freeway music to a pompous soundtrack for an oil company promo film, from country and western to Muzak. The main theme, which floats in and out of the film, is a beautiful guitar piece with a sweet keyboards backing.

Mark even assembled a *ceilidh* band for one sequence when he visited the set in Scotland in June. Ed Bicknell was on drums (though he's not seen in the film), Alan Darby from Fashion on guitar, Alan Clark on piano and a few locals on traditional instruments. The full soundtrack was recorded in New York in July and August.

It was a new and stimulating way of working for Mark: 'The difference between doing the soundtrack and a Straits album is that you're doing it for somebody else. It's not such a personal deal. It's good for you because they might turn round and say: "Well, I don't like that," and you think again. It's not usual for anyone in the band to say they don't like something.

'I think it's really good training and I'd like to do it again. But I'm still not sure whether I can do it. I think you have to do a few before you really get the hang of it. Like an idiot, I went off doing stuff far too early. It was just dumb, basically.

'They sent me rough early videos of the movie and, me being me, I went off doing music to these early videos, blithely ignoring the fact that they were going to cut the fuck out of the movie, which of course they did. Bill Forsyth told me: "I've decided to butcher every scene," so I went away and had to do a lot of it again. But it was great to do, because you can bring in all different sides of yourself, and bits of music that you've picked up, and bring it all together. You have to use your imagination a lot. And sometimes you have to dig fairly deep.'

The film was released in March 1983, to very favourable reviews. A single, 'Going Home', was released at the same time, and the soundtrack album appeared in April. As these things are, it's rather unsatisfactory divorced from the pictures on the screen, but is still an impressive collection of mellow themes of delicate beauty with Mark's guitar and Alan's keyboards the chief instruments.

By comparison with the band's albums, the music here is very simple, flowering out when other instruments are introduced, like Mike Brecker's sax on 'Going Home' and Gerry Rafferty's vocals on 'The Way It Always Starts', the only non-instrumental track. Dire Straits are featured on only one track, the zippy 'Freeway Flyer'. When seen with the film, however, the music becomes integral, highlighting the story, shading in the images.

From March to September 1982 Mark spent most of his time in the studios, recording *Love Over Gold* and *Local Hero,* back to back, with sessions for other artists in between – Stevie Nicks, Van Morrison, Phil Everly, the McGarrigle Sisters. In that period, Dire Straits lost another founder member: drummer Pick Withers.

Ed says: 'We don't really know why Pick left. I think it's a combination of reasons. It had been on the cards for a long time that he was unhappy with touring; not the playing, but the time spent away from home. During the making of *Love Over Gold,* Pick conceived in his mind certain things that I don't think have much foundation in fact – for instance, that drums no longer played an important part in Dire Straits. Another comment he made to me was that: "If I can't play drums with Weather Report, I'm going to give up."' Pick completed his work on the album and left the band on 23 June.

Mark says: 'He's in Wales with his baby and his wife and he wants to learn vibes and piano. He said he wasn't happy with his drums. Touring is tough. If we'd been eighteen when the first album started going nuts all over the world, we'd probably be lucky to be alive right now. I think it's only the fact that we had some semblance of sanity early on that we managed to get through it more or less intact.'

John agrees: 'One of the important things to remember is that when the band became successful, neither Pick nor David could handle it. Some people can. They take it for what it is, enjoy it and all the rest of it. But David was never happy with it, although he would love to be successful himself as a songwriter. Pick was the same. It's something that comes from your upbringing – you prefer to be the underdog, almost, rather than be on top.

'Mark and I really enjoy being successful – and I'm not talking about the money, I'm talking about the idea of success. And if you can't cope with it, then you have to get out of it, and that's what David and Pick did. Mark and I have ended up the only two members of the original band left, and I don't think that's any coincidence.'

Pick's leaving had been on the cards for a long time

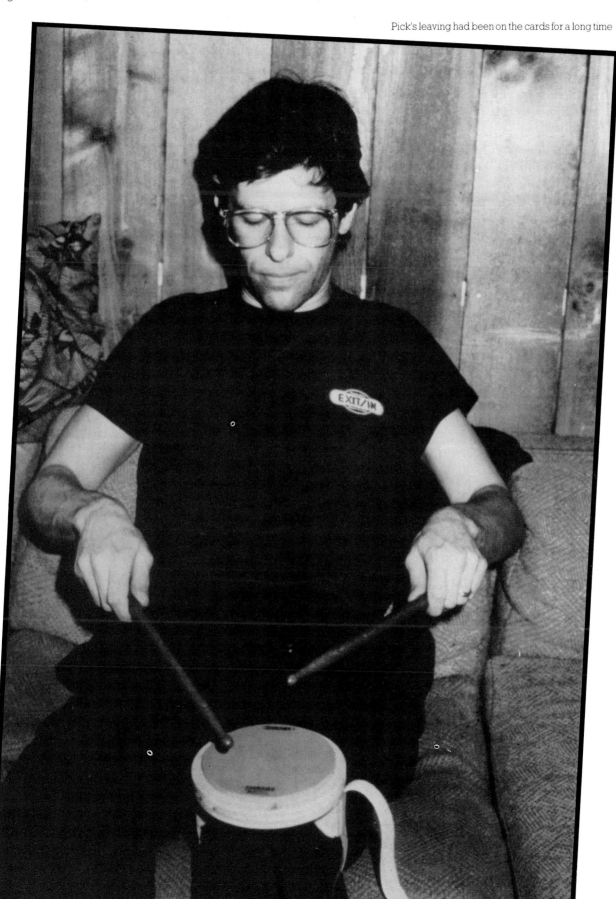

137

D I R E   S T R A I T S

The short-lived second quartet version of Dire Straits: promotion picture of Alan, Mark, John and Hal for *Love Over Gold*

A replacement for Pick was found in Terry Williams who, like his predecessor, is an experienced drummer steeped in rock 'n' roll. He is the son of a musician, and was born in January 1948 in Swansea. He started playing with a group at school and when he was fifteen his father bought him a drum kit. Terry joined a local group, the Commancheros, doing the inevitable Shadows covers until a singer arrived and the repertoire expanded to include rock and blues material.

In 1966 he turned professional with a local group, the Jets, which also featured Martin Ace and Deke Leonard. 'We went to Hamburg for a season at the Top Ten Club. That's where I got into jamming, because we'd play for hours . . . from seven in the evening until seven in the morning.'

On their return to Britain, the Jets split, but Terry went back to Germany for a four-month stint with the Bobcats, also with Martin Ace. This band later became the Dream, a club band which played all over Britain from 1967 to mid-1969. Then followed a spell with Dave Edmunds' band Love Sculpture, who had a hit single with a frenetic version of 'Sabre Dance', which took him on an American tour.

Returning from the States, Terry joined Man, which reunited him with Martin Ace and Deke Leonard. The group, heavily influenced by West Coast American rock, recorded several albums and singles and became one of Britain's most popular club bands during the early seventies, but they never made the breakthrough into the very top league.

When Man finally called it a day, Terry met up again with Dave Edmunds in Rockpile, alongside Nick Lowe and Billy Bremner, the quintessential good rockin', hard livin' British band of the late seventies and early eighties, bouncing along on the combination of Lowe's formidable talent for writing simple, catchy songs and Edmunds' ability to turn virtually anything into tight, danceable rock 'n' roll. But that band, too, split and Terry turned to sessions and contract work, latterly with Meat Loaf's travelling carnival.

Alan says: 'Terry has made a tremendous amount of difference. Obviously he's a very different kind of drummer to Pick, therefore he's going to make a heavy difference in the direction of the band. It's a matter of interpretation. Terry is a totally individual drummer, therefore he doesn't want to copy Pick.'

He came in at another peak. 'Private Investigations' was released before the album came out, and became the band's most successful single in Britain.

Partly to counter criticisms that the album was too gloomy, Mark decided to change mood for a follow-up single and returned to the straight-down-the-line rock 'n' roll of the early days, reviving 'Twisting By The Pool'. The band booked into Jam Studios in North London and in three days in October completed a three-track EP that recalled the days of the old shuffleboogie down at the Hope & Anchor: 'Twisting'; 'Two Young Lovers', a raving Chuck Berry pastiche; and 'If I Had You', an upbeat ballad. In February 1983 it became another Top Ten hit.

On 30 November 1982, the band started off their world tour in Guildford. It was broken in early spring to allow Mark time to fly to New York and co-produce a new album for Bob Dylan, *Infidels*—a welcome return to the biting edge of rock after the more ethereal style of Dylan's recent religious works. Alan went too, adding his

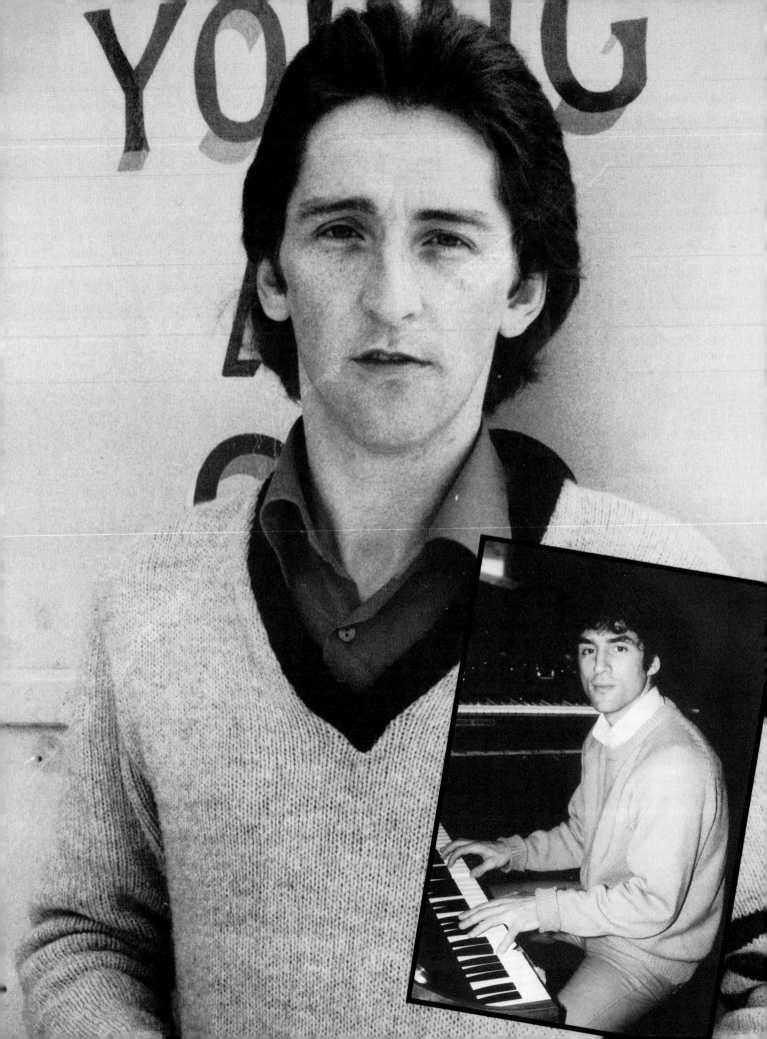

distinctive keyboard sound to the cast of renowned musicians assembled for the sessions.

All along it had been planned for the Straits tour to wind up with dates in Britain. The opportunity came when they were invited to play a royal charity gala in aid of the Prince Of Wales' Trust at the Dominion Theatre, London, before Prince Charles and Princess Diana (a long-time Straits fan). Also on the bill were Duran Duran, who were enjoying a peak of popularity at the time, and stole all the media attention. But on-stage, where it counts, the musical honours were won without question by Dire Straits.

The final dates came a few days later, when the band played two nights at London's Hammersmith Odeon: glorious end-of-tour parties which were recorded for a possible live album and also filmed. The set was virtually the same as when the tour started, but the months of playing it live had made each song a roaring, raucous room-shaker, delivered as ever with style and finesse but sounding like a whooping shout of glory. They were greeted with delirious delight by packed audiences.

As the band struck up the final number, 'Going Home', Hank Marvin and Bruce Welch, heroes of a local Newcastle boy who years before had pressed his nose up against a shop window and gazed at a Shadows guitar, came on stage and helped Dire Straits play out a triumphant tour.

For the band, the following months meant time to wind down, but for an ex-Strait it was the moment to launch a new career as a solo artist. In September, David Knopfler released a solo single, 'Soul Kissing', shortly followed by an album, *Release*.

David had spent the three years since leaving the band writing and producing material for both himself and others. Spurred on by the acquisition of a grand piano, which he found easier to work with than a guitar, and by the formation of his own company, Paris Records, David was doing it all again – though this time on his own terms. His album contains many echoes of the Straits, although with its mixture of songs and styles it takes a different direction from their recent recordings. On 'Soul Kissing', a transitory song that covers the period since leaving the band, John Illsley plays bass. And on 'Madonna's Daughter', which David describes as his version of 'Expresso Love', Mark contributes the pulsing rhythm lines. One other song, 'Little Brother', appears, lyrically, to be a reference back to the Straits, but David denies that it is about his relationship with Mark.

It's a memorable, entertaining and commercial album. Who knows: for David the big wheel might start turning all over again.

New blood: Tommy Mandel (inset) is added on keyboards for the *Love Over Gold* tour; Terry Williams replaces Pick Withers on drums

The Straits on *Top Of The Pops*

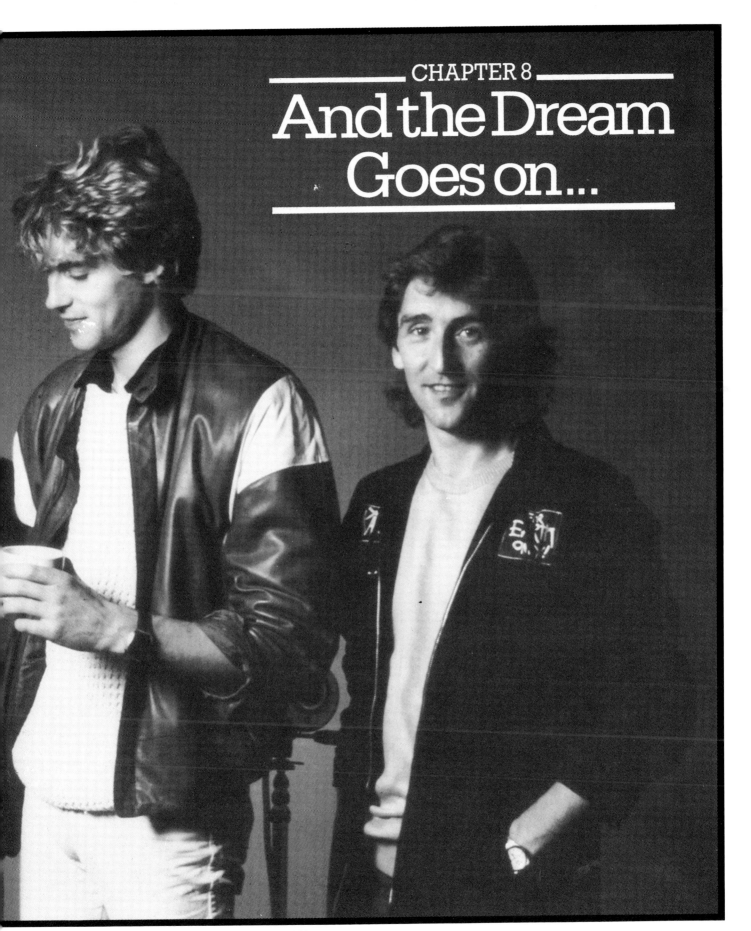

CHAPTER 8
And the Dream Goes on...

Mark, John, tour manager Paul Cummins, Alan, Hal, Terry Williams

Dire Straits are not the kind of band to spend a lot of time worrying about the future. Rock 'n' roll isn't like a bank; there's no career structure, no promotion, no company pension at the end of forty years' loyal service (though Dire Straits, with typical thoroughness, do have their own pension plan).

Individually, there are songwriting projects that may get to the recording stage, either inside or outside the structure of the band. Mark has designs on a soundtrack for a Western. He also wants to spend more time enjoying the fruits of his labours with his wife, Lourdes – they married in November 1983 – though with his capacity for work, that seems the most unlikely prediction of all.

They all have the vague feeling that sometime or another there must be a point when they will become parodies of themselves on-stage, old men playing their greatest hits to a hall full of pensioners. But there are older rock musicians than Dire Straits still playing, and keeping their credibility with a young audience.

Much depends on the music, and thus whether Mark can keep it fresh. 'I try to get better as a musician. I don't know whether I get any better as a writer at all. For instance, if you learn a new chord one morning out of a book, then as a writer I would straightaway start to use it.

'I just take advantage of that extra knowledge and put it to work. I don't actually have a hunger for musical training – I can't read music or anything – but everything I learn, I use. It means that you can advance. I'm really looking forward to the next few years. I keep falling in love with music all the time.'

Dire Straits are now at a stage where they're above musical fashion. It irks them somewhat that strangely-dressed mannequins can stand up on a stage, show a complete lack of any musical talent and yet grab all the headlines. But favour one day leads to disfavour the next. If Dire Straits aren't fashionable, then they can never go out of fashion. Better to keep their heads down and rely on the loyalty of those who like them for the music. There lies lasting success.

Everything they've achieved, Dire Straits have done for themselves. Every headline they've received has been earned by the strength and power of their music. They communicate their ideas without intermediaries building them up as personalities. They made their own breaks. Success has been their reward. In the process they have created music that will last long after the band has split or retired.

Mark, for one, though, will never give up. 'If I live to be sixty or sixty-five I can see me saying: "Well, dear, I'm just off to play with the lads." I'll walk into the pub on the corner and have a glass of wine or a beer with me mates and then we'll just play whatever it is we play. The way I'd like to grow old is to have an old band called the Sultans of Swing. I don't know what we'd be playing. We'd probably sound like a freaked out Weather Report. I can definitely see that happening.'

Check it out.

'Sure, Eric. My boy will write you a song.' Ed Bicknell and Eric Clapton backstage at Guildford at the opening of the *Love Over Gold* tour

Discography

Part One: Dire Straits

ALBUMS

DIRE STRAITS
Vertigo
June 1978
Side One
Down To The Waterline
Water Of Love
Setting Me Up
Six Blade Knife
Southbound Again
Side Two
Sultans Of Swing
In The Gallery
Wild West End
Lions
Personnel:
Mark Knopfler (vocals, lead and rhythm guitars)
David Knopfler (rhythm guitar)
John Illsley (bass)
Pick Withers (drums)
Producer:
Muff Winwood
Recorded:
Basing Street Studios, London, February 1978

COMMUNIQUÉ
Vertigo
June 1979
Side One
Once Upon A Time In The West
News
Where Do You Think You're Going
Communiqué
Side Two
Lady Writer

Angel Of Mercy
Portobello Belle
Single-Handed Sailor
Follow Me Home
Personnel:
Mark Knopfler (vocals, lead and rhythm guitars)
David Knopfler (rhythm guitar and vocals)
John Illsley (bass and vocals)
Pick Withers (drums)
Producers:
Jerry Wexler and Barry Beckett
Recorded:
Compass Point Studio, Nassau, Bahamas, December 1978
Mixed:
Muscle Shoals Sound, Sheffield, Alabama, January 1979

MAKING MOVIES
Vertigo
October 1980
Side One
Tunnel Of Love
Romeo And Juliet
Skateaway
Side Two
Expresso Love
Hand In Hand
Solid Rock
Les Boys
Personnel:
Mark Knopfler (vocals and guitars)
John Illsley (bass and vocals)
Pick Withers (drums)
Plus: **Sid McGinnis** (rhythm guitar)
Roy Bittan (keyboards)

Producers:
Jimmy Iovine and Mark Knopfler
Recorded:
The Power Station, New York, July–August 1980

LOVE OVER GOLD
Vertigo
September 1982
Side One
Telegraph Road
Private Investigations
Side Two
Industrial Disease
Love Over Gold
It Never Rains
Personnel:
Mark Knopfler (vocals and guitar)
Hal Lindes (guitar)
Alan Clark (keyboards)
John Illsley (bass)
Pick Withers (drums)
plus: **Mike Mainieri** (vibes and marimbas)
Ed Walsh (synth program)
Producer:
Mark Knopfler
Recorded:
The Power Station, New York, March–June 1982

SINGLES

SULTANS OF SWING/ EASTBOUND TRAIN

May 1978
Format:
7 inch
Personnel:
as *Dire Straits*

Producer:
Dire Straits
Recorded:
Pathway Studios, April 1978

ROMEO AND JULIET/ SOLID ROCK
November 1980
Format:
7 inch
Personnel, producer, studio:
as *Making Movies*

SKATEAWAY/ EXPRESSO LOVE
May 1981
Format:
7 inch
Personnel, producer, studio:
as *Making Movies*

TUNNEL OF LOVE
September 1981
Format:
7 inch
Personnel, producer, studio:
as *Making Movies*

PRIVATE INVESTIGATIONS/BADGES, POSTERS, STICKERS AND T-SHIRTS
August 1982
Format:
7 inch, 10 inch, 12 inch
Personnel, producer, studio:
as *Love Over Gold*

TWISTING BY THE POOL/ TWO YOUNG LOVERS/ IF I HAD YOU
January 1983
Format:
7 inch, 12 inch
Personnel:
Mark Knopfler (vocals and guitars)
Alan Clark (piano)
Hal Lindes (guitars)
John Illsley (bass)
Terry Williams (drums)
plus: **Mel Collins** (sax)
Producer:
Mark Knopfler
Recorded:
Jam Studios, London, October 1982

TRACKS ON COMPILATION ALBUMS

HOPE & ANCHOR FRONT ROW FESTIVAL
Warner Brothers
Track:
Eastbound Train
Personnel:
Mark Knopfler (vocals and guitar)
David Knopfler (guitar)
John Illsley (bass)
Pick Withers (drums)
Producer:
Dire Straits
Recorded:
Live at the Hope & Anchor, London, December 1977

THE HONKY TONK DEMOS
Oval
Track:
Sultans Of Swing
Personnel:
Mark Knopfler (vocals and guitar)
David Knopfler (guitar)
John Illsley (bass)
Pick Withers (drums)
Producer:
Dire Straits
Recorded:
Pathway Studios, London, June 1977

LOCAL HERO
Vertigo
Track:
Freeway Flyer
Personnel:
As for 'Twisting By The Pool'
Recorded:
London, September 1982

Part Two: Solo Work
MARK KNOPFLER

LOCAL HERO (album)
Vertigo
April 1983
Side One
The Rocks And The Water *(a)*
Wild Theme *(a)*
Freeway Flyer *(b)*
Boomtown (Variation Louis' Favourite) *(c)*
The Way It Always Starts *(d)*
The Rocks And The Thunder *(e)*
The Ceilidh And The Northern Lights *(f)*
Side Two
The Mist Covered Mountains *(g)*
The Ceilidh: Louis' Favourite, Billy's Tune *(h)*
Whistle Theme *(a)*
Smooching *(i)*
Stargazer *(e)*
The Rocks And The Thunder *(e)*
Going Home: Theme Of The Local Hero *(j)*
Personnel:
(a) **Mark Knopfler** (guitars, synthesizers, percussion, Linn drums)
Alan Clark (synthesizers, piano, Hammond organ)
(b) **Mark Knopfler**
Alan Clark
Hal Lindes (rhythm guitar)
John Illsley (bass)
Terry Williams (drums)
(c) **Alan Clark**
Mike Brecker (sax)
Mike Mainieri (vibes)
Neil Jason (bass)
Steve Jordan (drums)
(d) **Gerry Rafferty** (vocals)
Mark Knopfler
Alan Clark
Neil Jason
Steve Jordan
(e) **Alan Clark**
(f) **Alan Clark over The Acetones:**
Alan Clark (piano)
Alan Darby (guitar)
Roddy Murray (guitar)
Jimmy Yuill (whistle)
Mark Winchester (violin)
Dale Winchester (accordion)
Brian Rowan (bass)
Ed Bicknell (drums)
(g) **Alan Clark and Eddie Gomez** (bass) **over The Acetones**
(h) **The Acetones**

(i) **Mark Knopfler**
Alan Clark
Mike Brecker
Mike Mainieri
Tony Levin
(j) **Mark Knopfler**
Alan Clark
Mike Brecker
Tony Levin
Producer:
Mark Knopfler
Recorded:
Power Station, New York; Utopia/Eden Studios, London, July–September 1982

GOING HOME: THEME OF THE LOCAL HERO/ SMOOCHING (single)
March 1983
Format:
7 inch, 12 inch
Personnel, producer, studio:
as *Local Hero*

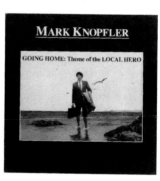

Sessions

BOB DYLAN
Album:
Slow Train Coming
Mark Knopfler:
guitar
Pick Withers:
drums

BOB DYLAN
Album:
Infidels
Mark Knopfler:
guitar, co-producer
Alan Clark:
keyboards

PHIL EVERLY
Album:
Phil Everly

Mark Knopfler:
guitar

PHIL LYNOTT
Album:
Kings Call
Mark Knopfler:
guitar

KATE AND ANNA McGARRIGLE
Album:
Love Over And Over
Mark Knopfler:
guitar

VAN MORRISON
Album:
Beautiful Vision
Mark Knopfler:
guitar

STEELY DAN
Album:
Gaucho
Mark Knopfler:
guitar

DAVID KNOPFLER

RELEASE (album)
Peach River Records
October 1983
Side One
Soul Kissing
Come To Me
Madonna's Daughter
The Girl And The Paper Boy
Roman Times
Side Two
Sideshow
Little Brother
Hey Henry
Night Train
The Great Divide
Personnel includes:
David Knopfler (guitar, keyboards)
John Illsley (bass on 'Soul Kissing')
Mark Knopfler (guitar on 'Madonna's Daughter')

SOUL KISSING/ COME TO ME (single)
Peach River Records
September 1983

Index

Page references in italic refer to illustrations

Photo Acknowledgments

The author and publishers are grateful to the following for permission to reproduce the illustrations on the pages listed:

Pages 1, US/PM (London Features International); 2–3, Graham Carne; 3 inset, Helen Oldfield; 4–5 (all pictures), Tom Sheehan; 6–7, Damage Management; 8–9, Tom Sheehan; 10–11 (both pictures), Tom Sheehan; 12–13 (both pictures), Tom Sheehan; 14–15 (both pictures), Tom Sheehan; 18–19 (all pictures), Tom Sheehan; 20–1, Tom Sheehan; 22–3, Tom Sheehan; 24–5 (both pictures), Tom Sheehan; 26–7, Tom Sheehan; 28–9, Helen Oldfield; 30–1, Barry Plummer; 32–3, Chris Horler; 33, Helen Oldfield; 34–5, Helen Oldfield; 36–7 (all pictures), Helen Oldfield; 38–9 (both pictures), Helen Oldfield; 40–1, Oval Records; 42–3 (all pictures), Helen Oldfield; 44–5, Helen Oldfield; 46–7, Chris Horler; 47, Helen Oldfield; 48–9, Rex Features; 50–1, Barry Plummer; 52–3 (both pictures), Barry Plummer; 54–5, Adrian Boot; 55, Adrian Boot; 56–7, (all pictures), Adrian Boot; 58–9, Chris Horler; 60–1, Chris Horler; 62–3 (both pictures), Adrian Boot; 64, Robert Legon; 65, Adrian Boot; 66, Robert Legon; 67, Adrian Boot; 68–9, (both pictures), Adrian Boot; 70–1, Robert Legon; 72–3, (both pictures), Adrian Boot; 74–5, (both pictures), Barry Plummer; 76–7 (both pictures), Barry Plummer; 78–9 top, Stephen F. Morley; 78–9 bottom, Adrian Boot; 80–1, Adrian Boot; 82–3, Adrian Boot; 84–5 (both pictures), Adrian Boot; 86–7, Adrian Boot; 88–9 (both pictures), Adrian Boot; 90–1 (both pictures), Adrian Boot; 92–3, Helen Oldfield; 94–5, Hal Lindes; 96–7, Damage Management; 99, Guido Harari; 100–1, Tom Sheehan; 102–3, Helen Oldfield; 104–5 (both pictures), Helen Oldfield; 108–9 (all pictures), Helen Oldfield; 110–11 (both pictures), Helen Oldfield; 112–13, Helen Oldfield; 114–15, Helen Oldfield; 116–17, Guido Harari; 117, Graham Carne; 118–19 (both pictures), Damage Management; 120–1 (both pictures), Graham Carne; 122, Graham Carne; 123, Tom Sheehan; 124–5 (all pictures), Tom Sheehan; 126–7, Tom Sheehan; 128–9 (all pictures), Guido Harari; 130–1 (both pictures), Guido Harari; 132–3 (both pictures), Guido Harari; 138, Phonogram; 140 main picture, Tom Sheehan; 140 inset, Pete Brewis; 142–3, BBC (London Features International); 144–5, Damage Management; 146–7, Damage Management; 148, Barry Plummer.